MW01049269

CHRIST|Life

ruthmyers

Multnomah® Publishers *Sisters, Oregon*

CHRIST/LIFE
published by Multnomah Publishers, Inc.

© 2005 by Ruth Myers
International Standard Book Number: 1-59052-395-4

Cover design by DesignWorks Group, Inc.
Cover art/photo by Steve Gardner, PixelWorks Studio.net
This book is not in any way associated with, affiliated with, or sponsored by ChristLife Catholic Evangelical Services.
Scripture quotations are from:
Holy Bible, New Living Translation (NLT) © 1996.
Used by permission of Tyndale House Publishers, Inc. All rights reserved.
New American Standard Bible®(NASB) © 1960, 1977, 1995 by the Lockman Foundation. Used by permission.
Revised Standard Version Bible (RSV) © 1946, 1952 by the Division of Christian Education of the
National Council of the Churches of Christ in the United States of America
The Amplified Bible (AMP) © 1965, 1987 by Zondervan Publishing House.
The Amplified New Testament © 1958, 1987 by the Lockman Foundation.
The Bible: A New Translation by James Moffatt (Moffatt) copyright 1950, 1952, 1953, 1954 by James Moffatt
The Holy Bible, *English Standard Version* (ESV) © 2001 by Crossway Bibles,
a division of Good News Publishers. Used by permission. All rights reserved.
The Holy Bible, New International Version (NIV) © 1973, 1984 by International Bible Society,
used by permission of Zondervan Publishing House
The Holy Bible, New King James Version (NKJV) © 1984 by Thomas Nelson, Inc.
The Holy Bible, King James Version (KJV)
The Holy Bible: The Berkeley Version in Modern English (Berkeley) © 1959 by Zondervan Publishing House
The Inspired Letters in Clearest English, Frank C. Laubach (Laubach) copyright 1956 by Thomas Nelson & Sons
The Living Bible (TLB) © 1971. Used by permission of Tyndale House Publishers, Inc. All rights reserved.
The Message © 1993, 1994, 1995, 1996, 2000, 2001, 2002 Used by permission of NavPress Publishing Group
The New Testament in Modern English (Phillips) © 1958 by J. B. Phillips
The New Testament: A Translation in the Language of the People, Charles B. Williams (Williams) copyright 1937
by Bruce Humphries, Inc., copyright renewed 1965 by Edith S. Williams, Moody Bible Institute
The New Testament in Modern Speech (Weymouth) © 1903, 1904, 1909, 1912 Translated by
Richard Francis Weymouth; edited and revised by Ernest Hampden-Cook.

Multnomah is a trademark of Multnomah Publishers, Inc., and is registered in the U.S. Patent and Trademark Office.
The colophon is a trademark of Multnomah Publishers, Inc.

Printed in the United States of America

For information:
MULTNOMAH PUBLISHERS, INC. • P.O. BOX 1720 • SISTERS, OREGON 97759

Library of Congress Cataloging-in-Publication Data
Myers, Ruth.
Christ/life / Ruth Myers.
p. cm.
ISBN 1-59052-395-4
1. Christian life. I. Title.
BV4501.3.M94 2005
248.4—dc22

2005003062

05 06 07 08 09 10—10 9 8 7 6 5 4 3 2 1 0

contents

PART THREE
THREE PILLARS OF YOUR NEW IDENTITY

WHO YOU
REALLY ARE...
at first

a CRUCIAL QUESTION

WHO ARE YOU?

Your deepest answers to that simple question are vitally important, because your thoughts and feelings about yourself determine the quality of your attitudes and actions.

This is true for all of us. A small self-image sets boundaries on what we can accomplish. A negative self-image predisposes us to failure and unhappiness. An inflated self-image makes us our own worst enemy in relating to other people.

And a *changed* self-image—one that is transformed by God—can alter our personality and behavior in delightful ways. That's what this book is about.

For several decades mainstream psychology has emphasized the importance of our self-image, the mental picture of ourselves that we carry around within us. But that's something the Bible has emphasized for centuries!

In the Bible, God gives Christians a new self-image, a new sense of identity. His work of changing us is not primarily directed to the outer margins of our lives, but to the very center. Through His Word and His Holy Spirit, He transforms us by renewing our minds.

At what moments do you find yourself longing for a fuller answer to the question "Who am I?" Why do we all seem to feel the need at times to better understand ourselves? (Feel free to jot down your thoughts here.)

GOD PUTS GREAT EMPHASIS on our self-concept because we act like the person we see ourselves to be. In this book we'll see how He expands our self-image as we allow Him to. This will broaden our view of what is really possible for us. He superimposes a glorious, positive self-image over our false and negative views of ourselves. This helps to make triumphant living possible.

God's truth sets us free from pride, insecurity, and other inhibiting negatives. This means we can become the unique person He designed us to be before our birth, when in the womb we were "intricately embroidered with great skill" (Psalm 139:14–15, paraphrased).

In revealing His truth to us, God teaches us to acknowledge the negatives about ourselves. From His point of view, everything we are "in the flesh"—even our self-attained righteousness—is corrupt. And He causes us to face another fact, one that is negative only from the viewpoint of human pride: our helplessness and inability, on our own, to achieve anything of value in His sight.

Admitting these humbling truths is essential. Without this we live in false self-confidence, relying on the ability of the flesh, which "profits nothing" (John 6:63).

But God doesn't stop with telling us about the negatives. He teaches us to dwell in the positive facts of who we are in Christ now and forever. Yes, we're to glance at the negatives, but we're to *focus* on the positives. This keeps us from wallowing in the weakness and sinfulness of our flesh.

"Be honest in your estimate of yourselves."
ROMANS 12:3, NLT

"Let us go on...advancing steadily toward the completeness and perfection that belongs to spiritual maturity."
HEBREWS 6:1, AMP

As you anticipate what you can learn in this book, talk with God about your personal commitment: (a) to be honest in your self-evaluation, and (b) to persevere in pressing toward spiritual, mental, and emotional maturity.

OUR QUEST FOR IDENTITY can sometimes occur on a low level, rooted in desiring a self-assurance that's independent of God. In contrast, He wants us to freely acknowledge our dependence on Him as we seek to discover who we are on the highest plane possible. Just think! God "has brought us into this place of highest privilege where we now stand, and we confidently and joyfully look forward to actually becoming all that God has had in mind for us to be" (Romans 5:2, TLB).

As we'll see, God created us to have a God-supported ego. We can gain an accurate sense of identity only as we're securely grounded in Him and His Word. He supports us with the confidence that, in Christ, each of us is "all right" as a person forever. Why? Because we share His belongingness, His worthiness, His competence.

The closer we walk with the Lord, the more vividly we'll learn to recognize both the negatives and the positives about ourselves. As we repeatedly acknowledge the negatives, then turn from them to believe the positives, our daily experience of who we are in Christ expands. The facts about our identity in Him become active forces in our lives by faith—by trusting the Holy Spirit to work within us.

And we strengthen our faith by practice—by accepting the truths God reveals and praising Him for them.

Pause for a moment to acknowledge to your heavenly Father how dependent you are on His help in better understanding your true identity. Let Him hear how much you look forward to all that He'll show you about yourself...and about Himself as well!

A Crucial Question

Use the following words to help you talk with your heavenly Father about the things you've been reading in these pages.

Who am I?
How I rejoice, Lord, that the answer to this question is known
so fully and intimately by You, my loving creator and Father!

I look to You, my gracious Lord, to continue revealing to me
who I am as You see fit, according to Your sovereign will.
You know fully what I need to understand about myself.
You know the distorted ideas and wrong labels in my
self-identity that need to be corrected.
Help me see these clearly.

Work in me, Lord, so that I will love and worship You more
and serve You better by choosing a more accurate self-image.
Transform me day by day through a fresh new awareness
of who You are and who I am in Your sight.

I ask this in Jesus' name, with deep gratefulness for His
sacrifice that has won me an intimate relationship with You.
I'm so grateful that I can bring my requests to You
and freely receive Your answers. Thank You!

How did men and women of the Bible go about reflecting on their personal sense of identity? For an outstanding and helpful example, look afresh at David's prayerful words in Psalm 139. As you read, ask yourself, "What truths especially minister to my sense of who I am?

OUR BEST MIRROR 2

To see ourselves, we need a mirror. That's true physically—and it's also true psychologically and spiritually, as we try to pin down who we really are as persons.

And what mirror do we use? Where do most of us turn for a clearer understanding of ourselves? Typically, it's the mirror of other people's opinions and their approval of our appearance, our performance, and our status. But such mirrors often reflect an image that is not only subjective, distorted, and unreliable, but also very changeable. When other people's smiles of approval are replaced by frowns of disapproval, it can quickly lead to anxiety, guilt, even hostility.

The ideal mirror is the mirror of God's love and truth as He has revealed them in His Word. As Christians we can open our Bible and find on its pages accurate insights into how God views us. It shows us God's total forgiveness, His perfect and limitless love for us, His constant supply of strength and encouragement, and His exciting purposes for our lives. These truths help us cultivate a new self-image—and they never change!

> The mirror of God's Word is a mirror of His love. "See how very much our heavenly Father loves us, for he allows us to be called his children, and we really are!" (I John 3:1, NLT, emphasis mine).

PHILIPPIANS 4:8 COMMANDS us to center our thoughts on things that are true, honorable, right, pure, lovely, commendable, excellent, and praiseworthy. We can apply these guidelines to the thoughts you and I have about ourselves.

It's in God's Word that we can find reliable and uplifting truths about ourselves, and dwelling on these truths can produce obedient, confident, and joyful living. We can think and know, "I'm clean through Christ's death on the cross. I'm free from the dominion of sin through His resurrected life. I'm competent to face life through His Spirit in me. I'm not expected to be a finished product now, but someday I will be. My destiny is to share His love, His purposes, and His glory now and forever!" Nothing gives us greater stability.

In reality, however, our lives are often shaky and faltering. We cower before our spiritual enemy; we feel discouraged and condemned. We feel we're in a deep hole and must somehow get ourselves out before any spiritual progress is possible.

Why do we feel like this? Because we're basing our self-image on (1) Satan's lies, (2) our own past experience, and (3) our feelings—instead of on the solid, glorious, scriptural *facts* of who God is, what He has accomplished, and who we are in Him.

Look closely at the guidelines given in Philippians 4:8 and think about them specifically in regards to your self-image, the way you routinely view and think about yourself. How well do your thoughts about yourself match these guidelines? Which of these guidelines do you feel can help you most?

> Whatever is true, whatever is honorable, whatever is just, whatever is pure, whatever is lovely, whatever is commendable, if there is any excellence, if there is anything worthy of praise, think about these things.
>
> PHILIPPIANS 4:8, ESV

YOU'LL HAVE OPPORTUNITY in this book to meditate on many Bible passages, giving God opportunity to "remold your mind from within" (Romans 12:2, Phillips). From these verses you can glean dynamic statements that will help you develop appropriate thought patterns—statements that will help subdue your defensive emotions and strengthen your positive ones. Whenever negative thoughts or emotions try to pull you down, God can use these statements to lift you more fully into the life of love, joy, and peace He has in mind for you.

So I encourage you to memorize the verses or phrases of Scripture that most help you believe that what God says about you is really true. Cultivate the habit of reaffirming these truths each time one of the negatives intrudes into your daily experience. Combat each intruder with Scripture.

In His Word God has graciously communicated to us the keys for developing an acceptable self-image that has unshakable supports. Using these keys, He wants to begin an inner "revolution" that will establish a new self-image. This can help inaugurate a new era in our lives—an era of inner strength and serenity as we face life in an insecure world. His truths about us give us a stable sense of "being somebody"—a solid inner platform of emotional security. From this platform we can relate more effectively to ourselves and others in every situation we face. His truths about Himself and about us provide on-the-spot strength to become more like Him in our daily lives and relationships.

Jesus once told a crowd, "Hear Me, everyone, and understand" (Mark 7:14).

As you seek to learn more about yourself by exploring God's viewpoint in the Scriptures, commit yourself to active, concentrated attentiveness to what He says. Listen closely…work hard to understand…and pray often that the Lord will teach you.

Our Best Mirror

REPEATEDLY IN PSALM 119 (NLT) the psalmist asked God to teach him so that he would live according to His Word.

Think about the following prayers from this Psalm. Let them stimulate you to pray with faith that God will be your counselor, as you study what He says about who you truly are.

"You made me; you created me.
Now give me the sense to follow your commands....
Open my eyes to see the wonderful truths in your law...." (vv. 73, 18).

"O LORD, the earth is full of your unfailing love....
Teach me, O LORD, to follow every one of your principles.... I will
delight in your principles and not forget your word" (vv. 64, 33, 16).

"I rejoice in your word like one who finds a great treasure....
As your words are taught, they give light; even the simple
can understand them.... Your word is a lamp for my feet and
a light for my path" (vv. 162, 130, 105).

"Let my lips burst forth with praise, for you have taught
me your principles" (v. 171).

God is qualified to teach you as you seek to embrace your true
and deepest identity. Mark any phrases in the above verses
that help you trust Him to do this.

Why can you trust God's Word to tell you what you most deeply need to know about your true identity? Discover the answers to that question which are indicated or implied in these passages:
John 6:63;
I Thessalonians 2:13;
Hebrews 4:12;
I Peter 1:23

SWAN STORY

REMEMBER THE OLD FAIRY TALE of the ugly duckling? A swan's egg was placed in a mother duck's nest. When her eggs hatched, one of the newborns stood out as different—awkward and gangly and oversized. He was quickly ridiculed by the other ducklings and soon felt inferior and excluded. Then one day he looked at his reflection in the water and made an amazing discovery—he had grown into a beautiful swan.

How confident are you that you truly can change, grow, and become more than you now are?

If the same situation occurred nowadays, the young misfit duckling would of course be taken to a professional counselor to undergo psychoanalysis. He might be told to simply adjust to the reality of being ugly and awkward and different. But that would mean ignoring a basic fact: He could change and grow and become more than he was. He could learn the dignity of assuming responsibility for his own future.

The ugly duckling in the story became a swan because of heredity. It was written in his genes before he was hatched. But the way people turn out is not quite so predetermined.

WHAT MAKES A HUMAN BEING'S personality unfold with all its potential grace and beauty? This depends on many subtle—or not so subtle—influences.

One factor is the person's environment. In a context of consistent emotional warmth, the personality blossoms with relative freedom. But the child may be deprived emotionally, in obvious or subtle ways. Or major experiences may intrude which make him feel rejected or abandoned. This may hinder the unfolding of his personality's unique beauty.

Another basic factor is our choices, our decisions to develop unhealthy thought and behavior patterns. Especially significant is the way we think about ourselves—our conscious thoughts and attitudes plus hidden feelings about ourselves that we lack the courage to face. Instead we labor to keep them submerged just below the level of consciousness.

Many of these patterns grew out of our initial basic conclusions about ourselves in our "duckling" stage. These conclusions were based on highly subjective impressions plus our limited ability to weigh the facts realistically. We grew up and never changed those faulty conclusions. We have failed to revise our inner data in the light of present reality.

So our present sense of identity may vary greatly from reality. And since we live like the person we see ourselves to be, the degree of fiction in our self-image severely limits our ability to live realistically, appropriately, and lovingly.

What limitations have you sensed in your ability to live realistically, appropriately, and lovingly?

PERHAPS ALL OF US EXPERIENCE a degree of self-rejection in some areas of our personalities, believing various illusions about ourselves. Our self-rejection may be total or partial, obvious or subtle, conscious or unconscious.

Regardless of how much or how little self-rejection we've experienced, we can't decide to simply overlook it and to accept ourselves arbitrarily, by pure willpower. We need valid grounds for deciding that our old self-rejection was a mistake, and that it's now realistic and appropriate to accept ourselves. We can't succeed in forming a more realistic sense of identity if, deep inside, we harbor beliefs that result in self-distaste or self-hate or marred relationships.

That's why the Bible is so valuable on this subject. It reveals God's truth about who we really are and provides reliable, unchanging grounds for accepting ourselves.

As we'll discover more fully, the Bible shows us the truth about ourselves. Each of us is (a) unique and wonderful, (b) flawed and morally guilty, and (c) fully dependent on God. Each of us has been uniquely engineered by God for success, but has also been given limitations and weaknesses. It's important therefore that we accept this full reality about ourselves, and not just the parts we like!

Accepting ourselves doesn't imply approving everything about ourselves. It means simply that we admit the kind of person we are—our gifts and strong points, our weaknesses and limitations, and our predominant needs.

What gifts and strong points in your personality are you most conscious of?

What personal weaknesses, limitations, and predominant needs are you most aware of?

What conscious forms of self-rejection do you find yourself experiencing?

Swan Story

Is it true? Can we really change and grow and become more than we now are?

Thank You, my God and my Creator,
for holding out to me the promise that I can
become more than I now am—that I can become more mature,
that I can expand my capacity to love and serve You and others.

Show me the truth about choices I've made that
have led to unhealthy thought patterns about myself—
thought patterns that limit me from being all that You
created me to be. Show me the right choices I can make
to break through these falsehoods and limitations.

Open my eyes to reality. More and more help me face up
to the full picture of who I truly am, both positives and negatives.
Open my eyes to the reliable, unchanging grounds
You have given for an accurate and liberating self-acceptance.

On this topic, explore the relevant messages from God's Word that you find in these passages:
Psalm 92:12–15;
Romans 8:29;
2 Corinthians 3:18;
Ephesians 4:15;
Colossians 1:10;
2 Thessalonians 1:3;
2 Peter 3:18

YOUR INNER
IDENTITY ALBUM

AM I SOMEBODY—or a nobody?

Is there hope of becoming more than I am?

And *why* am I here, anyway? Where am I going? What purpose can there be for me on this confused, polluted, violent planet where mankind may ultimately destroy itself, and perhaps soon?

Your instinctive responses to such questions flow from your deep-rooted sense of who you are—your self-image.

Psychologists have long recognized the self-image as the key to human personality and behavior. Most significantly, your self-image represents the value you place on yourself. It's your ideas and attitudes toward yourself, the feelings you have about who you are in relation to other people. When our self-image is threatened, we feel anxious, insecure, hostile, or guilty. When it is supported and intact, we feel confident and serene.

Your self-image is the picture (or series of pictures) of *you* that you carry in your mind. It's not like a photo that you could pull out and show others, but it reveals itself constantly in your attitudes, speech, and behavior.

As you think about the controlling pictures of yourself which are stored in your mind, what images from your past do you visualize first?

Do you have any fears about opening up these inner images for a closer inspection? If so, what is it that makes you fearful?

OUR PAST EXPERIENCES have produced in our minds mental images of ourselves—a sort of mental photo album that strongly influences our sense of identity. Some of the pictures are clear; others are blurry, out of focus, but still there.

Many of the pictures in this identity album have been produced by our past experiences in sin, self-will, and spiritual failure. We give these images a variety of "captions." Some of the captions might be excuses such as "I had to look out for my own rights" or "I had to do this *my* way" or "It was only a little sin."

Other captions represent powerful conclusions we've drawn about ourselves. They may read something like "I'm superior to others"—or "I'm inferior to others." They might state "I'm always right" or "I'm always doing or saying the wrong thing."

Through these images, our past often governs our present in a destructive, negative way. That's why this old identity album can never provide the ultimate, unshakable support we need for our self-image.

God, however, shows us how to "forget" the images from our past which hinder our spiritual and personal growth and undermine our self-image. We can revise our inner identity album and learn to use it constructively. God wants to transform our minds, filling them with a new self-image that's in line with His Word— an inner change that can revolutionize our personality and behavior

"I am focusing all my energies on this one thing: Forgetting the past and looking forward to what lies ahead, I strain to reach the end of the race and receive the prize for which God, through Christ Jesus, is calling us up to heaven."

PHILIPPIANS 3:13–14, NLT

What do you think might be some right ways and some wrong ways to go about "forgetting the past"?

We can't entirely erase the old, negative images in our inner identity album, but we can overpower them with something better. We can revise our album and learn to use it constructively. By deliberate choices we can open the album again and again and implant *positive* and realistic images that are in line with what God says about us.

We may have chosen long ago a lifestyle governed by untrue thoughts and feelings about ourselves—some negative, some arrogant and prideful. Our unhealthy thought and behavior patterns may be deeply habitual. But we can choose to change them. We *can* begin a process of significant growth, no matter where we are in life. We *can* take responsibility for building up a more accurate and positive sense of who we are from God's viewpoint.

To do this we must expose our minds to the facts God gives in the Scriptures about who we are. We can "develop" these true mental pictures of ourselves through meditating on the Scriptures and thanking God that they are true. The pictures will stay sharp and in focus as we continue to review and believe and use them.

God's Word will continue to throw light on the old, unrealistic pictures, so that we can acknowledge them honestly and stop being deceived by them. The more clearly we see ourselves from God's point of view, the more He motivates us to turn from our old false ways of viewing ourselves.

The task of revising your "inner identity album" and learning to use it constructively is a major undertaking. It involves a lengthy process of self-examination and careful attention to God's truth about who you really are. Will you stick with it?

Take a moment to articulate your willingness and eagerness for this task. Record your thoughts in the margins on this page.

Your Inner Identity

Thank You, Lord, for holding out to me the hope
of cultivating a stronger, more accurate self-image.

Thank You for Your commitment to sustain me in this process.
I'm grateful for the help and strength I can count on through
Your Holy Spirit who is at work in my heart and mind.

Thank You especially for the rich truths about myself that You've
inscribed in the pages of the Bible. How amazed I am that
these ancient words can be so personally on target
in describing me and helping me.

"Fear not, for I am with you; be not dismayed, for I am your God; I will strengthen you, I will help you, I will uphold you with my righteous right hand."

Isaiah 41:10, ESV

5
acknowledging wrong images

What are some unhealthy emotional reactions that reappear in your life in situations that are somewhat similar?

What are the common factors that seem to trigger this kind of response?

Consider how these unwholesome reactions might offer clues to some ingrained negative images about yourself.

To renovate our inner identity album, we must understand and acknowledge the unrealistic images that are there—and the harm they cause.

Our typical emotional reactions often serve as clues to negative images of ourselves that we need to reject or update. For example, someone may correct you, offering a suggestion that causes you to inwardly bristle. A possible reason: Your inner identity album has flipped open to the image of a perfectionistic authority in your past who kept peering over your shoulder and finding fault with your performance.

When something happens that triggers a replay of a former experience, we tend to react to the present situation as though it were the past one. Sometimes we consciously recall that scene from the past, but often we merely experience the emotion without remembering the exact original happening.

In various ways, it's easy for the negative images in our inner identity album to be triggered into our present consciousness, influencing our attitudes and behavior.

To HELP YOU BETTER understand your inner identity album, reexamine your viewpoints and beliefs.

It's possible you're holding on to some mistaken ideas about yourself and how you should live. Ask yourself, "Do I hold some basic beliefs that blind me to realities that don't fit my frame of reference? Could these beliefs be wrong?"

Do I have unrealistic beliefs about people? Such as: "There's no one you can trust." "All men are tyrants (or egotists, or slobs)." "All women are fickle (or featherbrained, or domineering)." "Don't let yourself grow really close in any relationship; in the end, you always get rejected and abandoned."

Do I have unrealistic beliefs about life? "If the circumstances are tough, they can't be good for me." "Avoid failure at all costs." "I need everyone to like me." "Life should be easier than this—it should go more smoothly."

And do I have unrealistic beliefs about God? "If I give Him full control, He'll take away my happiness." "All my suffering is God's fault." "My life matters nothing to Him." "If He really cared, He wouldn't have let these bad things happen to me."

We need to become more objective in our viewpoints and beliefs. We must learn not to color the facts with our misguided conclusions and opinions. For example, the fact may be, "I failed to accomplish this particular goal." But the statement, "So I'm just a failure," is unrealistic.

"Examine and test and evaluate your own selves...."

2 CORINTHIANS 13:5, AMP

Take enough time to seriously ponder each question listed in the text on this page.

What unrealistic or mistaken ideas or viewpoints or conclusions about yourself—or about other people or life or God—might you be holding on to?

ONE VERY COMMON TYPE of unrealistic thinking that needs replacing in most of our minds is this: "If only my situation would change, I'd feel better." Or, "If only my husband (or wife, or children, or parents, or employer) would change...." Or, "If only my past had been different...."

But as we'll learn throughout this book, we can replace those futile "if only" longings with reality, such as this thought: "I'm not at the mercy of my present circumstances or environment. My response to these things is always a matter of my own choice."

And this thought: "I'm not a slave to my past. The past contributed to what I am, but I can't change the past, only the present."

And this one: "I'm not willing to waste time waiting for others to change. I'm going to focus on how *I* can change, how I can develop new thought and behavior patterns."

You and I have the wonderful privilege and responsibility of rejecting all the unrealistic pictures in our inner identity albums. Then we can update our albums with realistic and liberating images, and use those images in ways that build up rather than tear down.

This will prepare us for greater enjoyment in our relationship with God, plus greater effectiveness in serving Him.

In what ways do you sometimes fall into "if only" thoughts like those listed in the first paragraph at the right?

Look closely at the more realistic thoughts suggested in the next few paragraphs. What can you do to respond more often with lines of thought like these?

Acknowledging Wrong

*Lead me, Lord, as I examine my viewpoints and beliefs and
how they affect my responses to situations and to people.
Help me do this in a firm and objective way.
Help me see the difference between the true facts
and my misguided opinions and conclusions.*

*Show me the traps I tend to fall into, and help me
understand why I'm so readily taken in by them.
And show me how I can learn to anticipate and avoid them—and how
I can replace my negative reactions with responses that please You.*

*Thank You for giving me this wonderful opportunity to identify
and reject the false pictures in my inner identity album.
Thank You for loving me enough to entrust me with the privilege
of updating my album with images that are accurate,
uplifting, and liberating—with truths about who
You are and who I am in Your sight.*

*Keep me on this path, Lord, so that in the days and months and years
ahead I may truly please You more and enjoy You in fresh ways.
I ask this in Jesus' name.*

How do the following passages indicate God's positive standards for us in examining and understanding ourselves? What encouragement do you find in these verses as you seek to develop a more realistic self-image?
Psalms 15:1–2; 51:6; 139:23–24; Proverbs 4:23; 14:8

Images

CHOOSING 6 new images

The freedom and
power of *choice*—what
an amazing gift our
God has given us!

Are you fully using this
power and freedom for
your spiritual growth…
especially in cultivating
a new self-image?

If you feel hesitant in
any way about this—
restricted, unable to
choose as freely as you
want—what exactly
is the nature of the
discomfort that you're
sensing? How can
you deal with what
you are feeling?

WE ARE FREE TO *choose* which pages of our inner identity album we want to focus on—on the ones that pull us down or the ones that lift us up. Each positive choice helps to update our sense of who we are and free us to change our attitudes and behavior and style of relating to people. More and more this lets the Lord transform us. It can also bring about gradual, positive changes in the attitudes of people toward us, and in the messages we receive from them that affect our sense of identity.

Choosing to develop realistic images of ourselves will mean giving up our evasions and admitting our need to change. It will mean learning to close those pages in our album that trigger discouragement or hostility or a tendency to blame others—and to open pages that make us grateful for all that God has done for us.

So when a situation arises that triggers an unrealistic image, we simply decide to turn the page. When we feel the undertow of negative thoughts and emotions, we reject the temptation to lock our focus on the negative pages, and instead we grab the "life raft" of positive images and focus on those.

ON SOME OF THOSE pages in our inner identity album, God wants us to add the labels "Unrealistic" and "Do Not Use."

On other pages, He wants us to use the headings "Realistic" and "Use Often." These realistic pages include not only the positive and uplifting facts that inspire and motivate us, but also the unappealing-but-true facts that humble us in helpful ways.

As we recognize these humbling pictures of our flaws and weaknesses, it helps to tell ourselves in a nondefensive way, "I have basic limitations and weaknesses, but so do all people. In many ways I need to change, but this isn't the final picture. I'm going to become more than I am. I'm far from perfect, but I don't need to be ideal or even almost perfect in order to be likable and acceptable right now."

So we admit the realistic negatives, then go on to focus on the positives, just as Paul advised the Christians in ancient Greece: "Fix your thoughts on what is true and honorable and right. Think about things that are pure and lovely and admirable. Think about things that are excellent and worthy of praise" (Philippians 4:8, NLT).

Let's say with the Psalmist, "I have chosen the way of truth" (Psalm 119:30, NKJV). And let's obey Paul's words to us, "Examine everything carefully; hold fast to that which is good" (1 Thessalonians 5:21, NASB).

What are some of the pages in your inner identity album on which it's likely that your heavenly Father wants you to add the labels "Unrealistic" and "Do Not Use"?

Which pages will God likely want you to mark "Realistic" and "Use Often"? Do you have enough of these pages? Do you need to add more? If so, this book will help you do just that!

YOU CAN BEGIN ADDING new, realistic snapshots into your inner identity album by developing realistic, positive ways of thinking. Feed into your memory truths about yourself that replace the unrealistic negatives you've decided to reject.

Select clear, positive statements that affect you in a positive way emotionally—especially Bible quotations that uplift you. Go over these statements again and again, to make a deep imprint in your brain. Do this emphatically and frequently, with thanksgiving.

In addition, let your positive memories work for you: the times you've felt loved or loving; the moments you have felt glad and hopeful; the good feeling you experienced over some success (even a small one).

Enlist your mind, emotions, and will in this. Choose to do it often and with feeling, in order to place an increasingly clear new image in your mental album. Do this with thanks to the Lord.

Whenever we're tempted to respond to a situation out of anxiety or without love, it's important not to wait for our inner attitudes or emotions to change before we respond more appropriately. If we begin to make realistic choices in our thought and behavior patterns, our emotions and attitudes will eventually fall in line. If we act the way we *want* to feel, our behavior patterns can begin molding our feelings.

> "Whatever you choose to obey becomes your master."
> ROMANS 6:16, NLT

At this time, what is your strongest motivation for wanting to build a realistic and positive new self-image that conforms more and more to God's intentions?

Are you confident that this can be done?

If not, say often with Paul, "I can do all things through Christ who strengthens me" (Philippians 4:13, NKJV).

Choosing New Images

Elihu, the wisest (and youngest) of Job's counselors, reminded him of this: "We can choose the sounds we want to listen to; we can choose the taste we want in food; and we should choose to follow what is right" (Job 34:3–4, TLB).

Thank You, heavenly Father, for the limitless freedom You have given me in Christ to choose what is good and right.

Thank You that this freedom extends deep within my inner being, even to the ways I view myself, which are often so heavily influenced by unhealthy patterns from the past. I count on You to give me the freedom to choose healthier, more realistic patterns of viewing myself— patterns that honor You as my Maker.

Day by day and hour by hour, help me learn to think wisely when I think about myself. Train me in this discipline of realistic thinking. Let me waste less and less time and energy and emotional vigor through ways of thinking that are flawed and faulty. Strengthen me to make wise mental choices.

Mighty God, I look to You and Your power to accomplish these things in me. "You are my strength and my shield; my heart trusts in You, and I am helped" (Psalm 28:7, NIV, personalized).

Following what is right includes believing who we are according to God, as David did in Psalm 23.

David saw himself as a sheep cared for by an ideal shepherd. Put yourself in David's sandals. What truths about yourself does this psalm reveal?

WHO I am as a CReated BeInG

Knowing the truth about our identity begins with a better grasp of who we are as created beings—a better understanding of the God-intended qualities each of us shares with all mankind. Rejoice in the following truths.

Simply because I am a human being created by God, I have capacities and potential abilities that can lead to a rich life of expansiveness and dignity. I have the ability…

—to know who I am and become more than I am.

—to think, to reason, to ponder, to grasp the meaning of reality, and to plan.

—to design and create such things as material objects, art, ideas.

—to make significant choices and to act in productive ways that can contribute to the well-being of others in large or small ways.

—to love—and thereby alleviate suffering and encourage the unfolding of the powers of other people.

Most significantly, I have a spirit—an inherent kinship with God who is Spirit, a potential for personally relating to Him.

Think about the marvelous dignity and extraordinary potential that belong to you and to every person around you simply by virtue of belonging to the human race.

As you consider the human abilities and capacities listed to the right, what effect could this have not only on how you view yourself, but also on how you view others?

BY GIVING ME A SPIRIT, God has designed me with the capacity to delight in His presence and taste His reality in the core of my being. I'm a valued person with whom God longs for loving involvement, not primarily for what I can do but simply for who I am. As a unique person I can bring Him pleasure in unique ways.

For each of us, this potential spiritual capacity can become reality in a living relationship with God. He gives us spiritual life through a new birth when we choose to trust Christ as our Savior.

But this living, loving relationship doesn't develop automatically. A satisfying love relationship with God, as with anyone, demands time and teamwork. It must be cultivated, often at the cost of eliminating seemingly important personal interests that are of lesser value. This requires more than a casual, lukewarm, haphazard approach to Him.

It's not enough merely to *decide* to love God more. We must also choose to behold Him in the Scriptures, letting His love for us permeate our inner being, break down our defenses, and draw out our warm response.

Just as a delightful awe floods our hearts when we see a brilliant sunset, so love for God rises back to Him when we take time to see what He is like and to let Him love us.

As you seek to grow in embracing God's truth about your identity, be sure to set apart adequate time to cultivate a satisfying love relationship with the Lord. If you sense that God wants more of your time for this, where can you include it in your schedule?

MANY PEOPLE SEEK to improve their self-image through the power of positive thinking (often a mixture of fact and fiction), and by self-improvement. Although improving our God-given abilities is wise, this is not the true basis for a stable sense of identity.

Instead we're to look to God's Word, for the truth about our identity is one of the basic messages woven into the fabric of Scripture. What God says about us goes hand in hand with what He says about Himself. Together, these truths about God and us can help move our inner being toward positive emotions and positive pictures in our inner identity album. More and more these truths will displace the defensive and depressing emotions that are part of the destructive effects of sin—including guilt, alienation, hostility, loneliness, frustration, discouragement, anxiety, despair, and lack of purpose.

The result for us will be a growing capacity to love both God and people—a capacity that will exceed anything we've ever known. C. S. Lewis expresses it this way in *Mere Christianity:*

What would you say are the basic differences between relying merely on "the power of positive thinking" and the transformation of your self-image that this book speaks of?

> The happiness which God designs for His higher creatures is the happiness of being freely, voluntarily united to Him and to each other in an ecstasy of love and delight, compared with which the most rapturous love between a man and a woman on this earth is mere milk and water.

The captions God writes in our new inner identity album will always include this one: "You were created for a love relationship with Me."

Who I Am as a

As we think about strengthening our loving relationship with God, we have many good reasons (and more will be added!) for praying the following words from A. W. Tozer, in *The Pursuit of God*:

"O God, I have tasted Thy goodness,
and it has both satisfied me and made me thirsty for more.
I am painfully conscious of my need of further grace.
I am ashamed of my lack of desire.

"O God, the Triune God, I want to want Thee;
I long to be filled with longing; I thirst to be made more thirsty still.
Show me Thy glory, I pray Thee, so that I may know Thee indeed.
Begin in mercy a new work of love within me.
Say to my soul, 'Rise up, my love, my fair one, and come away.'
Then give me grace to rise and follow Thee up from
this misty lowland where I have wandered so long.

"In Jesus' Name, Amen."

By reviewing closely the following passages, what deeper insights can you gain about who we are as created beings?
Genesis 1:26–29; 5:1–2;
Psalms 8:3–9; 100:3;
Isaiah 64:8;
Acts 17:26–28;
Romans 1:19–20

Created Being

made for god,
made for love

PEOPLE IN LOVE often say, "We were made for each other." This is far more true of us and our Creator than of any other relationship. We were made for Him! As C. S. Lewis explains it in *Mere Christianity,* "He Himself is the fuel our spirits were designed to burn, or the food our spirits were designed to feed on. There is no other."

God formed each of us for Himself, for His enjoyment as His special work of art, created to resemble Him. The Lord doesn't make His works of art to sell them. He makes them for His own permanent ownership—treasures that He continually enjoys as they respond to Him. He created them for an *abiding* relationship with Himself—for day-by-day fellowship and empowering, to His glory.

God is the initiator in this love relationship. "He has won me by His grace," one songwriter says with awe. And God continues to court us, always seeking the undivided love of our hearts.

> "What is man, that you make so much of him, and that you set your heart on him, visit him every morning and test him every moment?"
>
> JOB 7:17–18, ESV

How conscious are you of God's active "courting" of you? Through what actions and circumstances and messages is He signaling to you that He longs for your undivided love?

IN ANY CLOSE RELATIONSHIP, two questions are in our minds, consciously or unconsciously begging for answers.

First: *What is he (or she) to me?* How important is he to me? What needs of my heart and life will he meet? And second: *What am I to him?* What feelings and attitudes toward me can I depend on? How important am I to him? What needs of his can I meet?

We can apply these questions to our relationship with God. The answers to both of them gauge the depth of satisfaction and intimacy that our relationship with Him will bring. Let's consider the second question.

What am I to God? How can a self-existent, self-sufficient God "need" me? Does He just want to "use" me for His ends, at the cost of my true interests? What could I possibly give Him? For all things come from Him, and anything I "give" Him is already His.

Right now, with your present understanding, how would you answer these two questions: *What is God to me? What am I to Him?*

The word *need* can be defined as "anything required, *desired,* or useful." God is love, and love desires love in return.

In this sense, God's "need" for my love is shown in the commandment He rates as most important: "You shall love the LORD your God with all your heart, and with all your soul, and with all your mind, and with all your strength" (Mark 12:30, NASB). This is the most flattering verse in the Bible. God—altogether desirable, the Supreme Ruler of all—longs for my undivided love!

LOVE IS VULNERABLE. It seeks pleasure in its object, and it can be grieved by the response it gets.

The same is true with God's love for each of us.

If we don't respond to God, He will be "poorer," less satisfied, for it's in our power either to delight Him or to grieve Him—to bring Him joy or sorrow. "Every soul," A. W. Tozer reminds us, "is a vast reservoir from which God could receive eternal pleasure." It's like the pleasure the bridegroom receives when the bride accepts his love and offers her undivided devotion in return.

We delight God when we thankfully receive and enjoy all that He is to us, consenting to increased intimacy and involvement with Him. Then we have the inner resource of His presence and love and power, so that we can "live in a way worthy of the Lord and to His entire satisfaction" (Colossians 1:10, Berkeley).

Developing our relationship with God will increase our ability both to love people and to be loved by them—to unmask ourselves and open ourselves to closer relationships. It will also release us to become more than we are—to make our unique contribution, to exercise our special creative abilities, and to enjoy life on a new level.

It has been said that we get out of life that which we truly *want*. Ask yourself, "How seriously do I want to enjoy God's love and to return to Him the total love of my heart? Are there areas of life in which I'm holding Him at arm's length? Do I need to say 'Yes' to Him on some specific issue? Do I need to set apart a specific time of day and spend it regularly with Him alone?"

Made for God,

*You created me for Yourself! Thank You, Father,
for this astonishing truth that encompasses my life's
full purpose and significance and worth.*

*Unfold this truth to me more and more, so that I can recognize more
fully the meaning and guidance it gives to me in the everyday
circumstances of my life. I especially give You thanks for Your relentless
pursuing of my heart, and for sparing absolutely no cost in this pursuit.
In Jesus, Your Son, You have courted me and won me.
I am Yours and You are mine!*

*I acknowledge—with amazement—that You desire my love in response.
You invite me to love You with all my heart and all my soul and all my
mind and all my strength. I pray that more and more You will inspire
me and enable me to do this, for You, my loving God, are infinitely
worthy of such a response! Help me to grow day by day in offering You
my love more fully, and may I grieve or disappoint You less and less.*

*Today, may I gratefully receive and enjoy what You are to me,
and live more worthily of Your love. Keep taking me to higher levels
of knowing You and bringing joy to Your heart.*

What further whispers of God's personal love for you can you hear and enjoy in the following passages? John 4:23; 17:23; Romans 8:38-39; Ephesians 1:4–5; 2:4–7; 2 Thessalonians 2:16–17

Made for Love

too high or too low?

By exploring God's truth about who we are as created beings, we quickly expose the unrealities behind two of the basic kinds of masks people wear—two of the basic illusions that ensnare us.

Some wear mainly the mask of superiority. They say in effect, "I'm strong, talented, attractive, intelligent, important, or capable (or all of the above). Admire me!" This type of mask tries to hide weaknesses or needs.

This illusion of being superior and self-sufficient blinds a person to his total need for God. And such an inflated view predisposes us in a subtle way to defensive emotions. Being unrealistic, this tendency needs constant defense against the sword thrusts of reality.

For example, behind our anxiety may lie the belief (though perhaps unrecognized), "I'm the chief actor in my situation—it all depends on me." Yet beneath this inflated view lurks the question, "Am I really up to this?" And lurking behind our hostility is often this unspoken belief: "I'm the most important person—everything should center in me. I should have my way—I'm obviously right."

Behind any fear or anxiety or hostility that you may have experienced recently (or are battling even now), is it possible that lurking in you is an attitude of superiority or unrealistic self-sufficiency?

> I warn everyone among you not to estimate and think of himself more highly than he ought—not to have an exaggerated opinion of his own importance.
>
> Romans 12:3, AMP

OTHERS ON THE WHOLE wear the mask of inferiority. They say, or at least feel, "I'm weak, insignificant, insecure, incapable. I don't measure up. Sympathize with me! Reassure me!" This type of mask covers up their strong and positive traits.

Having too low a view of ourselves (just like having too exalted a view) sets the stage for hostile feelings. Why? Because it triggers inner reactions that confirm our low opinion of ourselves, whereas we long for the opposite. Or it feeds the fear that people will see what we are like and reject us. Or it results in self-punishment or in holding back in fear from responsible, creative, loving involvement.

Moreover, if we strongly dislike who we are, we'll find it difficult to truly love others.

Those who are caught in this illusion of being nobody, of being insignificant and meaningless, may still maintain, "I'm my own person, and whether right or wrong, I have a right to be me!" That's because, in both self-pride and self-pity, our "flesh" is central. In both we're following the dictates of the sinful nature and experiencing the destructive effects of sin.

When we sustain an unrealistic view of ourselves—be it self-exalting or self-effacing—we either intensify our dark emotions or force them underground where they function as traitors. Yet God sees it all.

> Even the darkness hides nothing from You, but the night shines as the day; the darkness and the light are both alike to You.
>
> PSALM 139:12, AMP

In what kind of circumstances are you most tempted to see yourself as weak, insignificant, insecure, or incapable?

Or strong and superior?

If you can think of people in your life whom you find particularly hard to love...could this inability somehow be related to a negative self-image in some area of your life?

MANY OF US VIEW ourselves too highly in some areas and too lowly in others. Actually, depending on the circumstances we're in, each of us is prone to respond with strength at times and with weakness at other times. That's because all of us are basically more alike than we tend to believe. In his book *The Strong and the Weak*, Paul Tournier explores the underlying universal weakness and fear experienced by *all* people—by those coming across as fearless and strong as well as those who seem anxious and fragile.

In what areas of life are you most likely to view yourself too highly?

To be *realistic* in the way we view and accept ourselves—that's the challenge.

To see ourselves realistically—and therefore to live realistically—we must recognize our position, our capacities, and our limitations as created beings. Illusions about ourselves provide unstable foundations for our emotional life, whether those illusions involve a self-exalting superiority or a self-belittling inferiority that fails to honor God as a good and wise Creator.

In what areas might you tend to view yourself too lowly?

God wants us to ground our inner beings in reality. Therefore He provides antidotes in His Word for both too high and too low a view of ourselves, as we'll soon see. His view of us isn't hindered by our pretenses; He sees right through the masks we wear. He knows all about people in general and each of us in particular. He sees the "whole package"—negative as well as positive—and yet accepts us unreservedly if we belong to Christ.

Too High or

❦

"Search me, O God, and know my heart! Try me and know my thoughts! And see if there be any grievous way in me, and lead me in the way everlasting!" (Psalm 139:23–24, ESV).

Dear Lord, I live in a fallen world where each of us, during at least part of our life, has been separated from You, our true source of identity. Often we have compensated for this with fictions about ourselves that make us feel valuable and important—or at least less left out. Thank You that You are faithfully at work to expose those negative fictions and replace them with positive truths! I ask You to do this more and more in my life.

How glad I am, Lord, that in doing this Your purpose is not that I should end up with a low, negative view of who I am. You rip away my unrealistic sense of importance or lack of importance in order to replace it with a sense of value and significance that's grounded in reality. With Your left hand You take away my phony inflated or deflated temporal self-image...and with Your right hand You give me back a true and eternal and uplifting knowledge of who I am.

Thank You, Lord, for Your unspeakable grace and mercy in helping me more and more to see myself from Your point of view.

Look afresh at the brief story Jesus tells us about two men in Luke 18:9–14. From the limited information Jesus gives, how would you assess each man's self-image?

Too Low?

a self-opinion too high

10

WHEN WE EXPLORE the Scriptures to see who we are in God's sight as His created beings, we discover a vast array of realistic new images for our inner identity album. Many of them serve especially as an antidote for having too high an opinion of ourselves; others are the exact remedy we need for a self-image that's too low.

Make time to reflect deeply on these biblical truths. They will provide trustworthy pictures and captions for your who-am-I album. They will help ground you in reality.

Helping to balance our sense of superiority will be this truth: *I'm infinitely less than God; compared to Him, I'm tiny in size, in importance, and in influence.* David expressed this truth so well: "When I look at the night sky and see the work of your fingers—the moon and the stars you have set in place—what are mortals that you should think of us, mere humans that you should care for us?" (Psalm 8:34, NLT).

Why do you think it's healthy for you to consciously and realistically compare yourself with God's attributes and character? What benefits does this provide you?

Do not become proud, but stand in awe.

ROMANS 11:20, ESV

"God…holds in His own power your breath of life and all your destiny."

DANIEL 5:23, MOFFATT

ACCURATE CAPTIONS like the following will also help us correct a self-opinion that's too high:

I'm short lived and transient. "What, after all, is your life?" the Scriptures ask. "It is like a puff of smoke visible for a little while and then dissolving into thin air" (James 4:14, Phillips). So we can learn to pray with David, "My whole lifetime is but a moment to you" (Psalm 39:5, TLB). And with Peter we can admit these words: "People are like grass that dies away" (1 Peter 1:24, NLT).

I'm under God's rule, under His sovereign power. "No one can stop him or challenge him, saying, 'What do you mean by doing these things?'" (Daniel 4:35, NLT). So we can kneel and pray, "Yours is the dominion, O LORD, and You exalt Yourself as head over all.... You rule over all, and in Your hand is power and might" (1 Chronicles 29:11–12, NASB). God is the One who "controls your destiny" (Daniel 5:23, NLT).

I receive everything from God. This is true regardless of whether or not we're conscious of it—and most of us need frequent reminders. Paul asked the Corinthians, "What do you have that God hasn't given you?" (1 Corinthians 4:7, NLT). And in proclaiming the one true God, Paul told the philosophers of Athens, "He himself gives to all mankind life and breath and everything.... For 'In him we live and move and have our being'" (Acts 17:25, 28, ESV).

Carefully evaluate your habitual attitudes. When does it seem easiest for you to forget that your life is very short, or that you live all of it under God's sovereign control, or that everything you have is a gift from God?

FACING UP TO the following facts can also help provide a reality check if we tend to feel superior or self-sufficient:

I'm accountable to God—responsible for my choices and behavior. For "God will judge us for everything we do, including every secret thing, whether good or bad" (Ecclesiastes 12:14, NLT). "Remember that you can't ignore God and get away with it" (Galatians 6:7, NLT).

I need God's guidance. As Jeremiah once prayed, "I know, LORD, that a person's life is not his own. No one is able to plan his own course" (Jeremiah 10:23, NLT).

I was designed to live totally by God's enabling. "Not that we are sufficient of ourselves...our sufficiency is from God" (2 Corinthians 3:5, NKJV).

Apart from God, my activities in life are ultimately empty of meaning. The author of Ecclesiastes devoted himself "to search for understanding and to explore by wisdom everything being done in the world." Then he came to this conclusion: "Everything under the sun is meaningless, like chasing the wind" (Ecclesiastes 1:13–14, NLT).

And finally, this all-important fact: *I'm a member of a fallen humanity—guilty and flawed.* As the prophet Isaiah confessed, "All we like sheep have gone astray; we have turned, every one, to his own way" (Isaiah 53:6, NKJV).

The words of C. S. Lewis sum up our situation well: "Our whole being by its very nature is one vast need; incomplete, preparatory, empty yet cluttered, crying out for Him who can untie things that are now knotted together and tie up things that are still dangling loose."

> "Proud man! Frail as breath! A shadow! And all his busy rushing ends in nothing."
>
> PSALM 39:5, TLB

> "For if anyone thinks himself to be something, when he is nothing, he deceives himself."
>
> GALATIANS 6:3, NKJV

A Self-Opinion

I freely acknowledge before You, my Creator,
these humbling facts about myself:

While You are infinite in capacity and power,
I am strictly and severely limited.
You are eternally existent—"from everlasting to everlasting,
You are God" (Psalm 90:2, NKJV)—while I am a breath,
a passing vapor that appears for a little while and then
vanishes away (James 4:14).

You are Lord and Possessor of all—and there's nothing I can keep or
hold or even touch that isn't a gift from You.
You are fully in control of the universe and everything in it,
of every detail, from the celestial sweep of galaxies to the slightest
movement of the smallest subatomic particles. There's no choice I can
make, no action I can take, that isn't subject to Your physical and
moral laws and principles, as well as Your sovereign will.
When I do my own thing, sooner or later I'm the loser.
It doesn't pay to disobey!

And I acknowledge before You that all this is not only the way
things are...but the way they should be!

According to the truths God gives us in the following passages, why is it so important to reject any inflated or arrogant aspects of my self-image?
Proverbs 11:2; 16:18–19; 18:12; 26:12; 29:23; Isaiah 2:11–12, 17; Matthew 23:12; James 4:6–7, 10

Too High

a seLf-OPINION too Low

11

"God did not create a standard person and in some way label that person by saying 'this is it.' He made every human being individual and unique.... You are not 'like' any other person and can never become 'like' any other person. You are not 'supposed' to be like any other person and no other person is 'supposed' to be like you.... 'You' as a personality are not in competition with any other personality simply because there is not another person on the face of the earth like you, or in your particular class.... You are not 'inferior.' You are not 'superior.' You are simply 'you.'"

MAXWELL MALTZ,
PSYCHO-CYBERNETICS

THROUGHOUT THE SCRIPTURES we can find truths that are the best antidote for having too low an opinion of ourselves.

One of the strongest of these is the fact that *each of us is a special, unique creation of God.* Designed by His skilled artistry, each person is a wonderfully unique entity who will never be duplicated, and who was never meant to be exactly like anyone else. Therefore we can joyfully and gratefully acknowledge to God, "Your hands have made and fashioned me" (Psalm 119:73, ESV). We can worship Him with David's words: "I praise you, for I am fearfully and wonderfully made" (Psalm 139:14, ESV).

A sense of this uniqueness helps us avoid the trap of constantly comparing ourselves with others. Paul speaks of those who "measure themselves by their own standards or by comparisons within their own circle," then adds, "and that doesn't make for accurate estimation, you may be sure" (2 Corinthians 10:12, Phillips).

"Your hands have made me and fashioned me, an intricate unity."

JOB 10:8, NKJV

WE NEED TO remind ourselves often of the following truths. Embracing them can help provide a reality check to use whenever we feel inferior or worthless or insignificant.

As a human being, *I'm a member of an exalted part of God's creation.* David confessed, "For you made us only a little lower than God, and you crowned us with glory and honor. You put us in charge of everything you made, giving us authority over all things" (Psalm 8:5–6, NLT). Each of us has an intrinsic value that far exceeds that of animals and inanimate things, however highly they may be treasured or valued in the home or in the marketplace.

I've been created in God's image. "So God created man in his own image, in the image of God he created him; male and female he created them" (Genesis 1:27, NIV). Dr. Maurice Wagner reminds us, "God created man in His own image so that man could be like God. He created me in His image so that God and I could walk together, enjoy each other, in a sense inhabit each other, occupy the same space in a living relationship important to both."

Even more amazing, *I'm dearly loved by God.* He has proven this by giving us His Son. "God demonstrates his own love for us in this: While we were still sinners, Christ died for us" (Romans 5:8, NIV). And He assures us, "You are precious in my eyes, and honored, and I love you" (Isaiah 43:4, ESV).

If you ever struggle with feeling inferior or worthless or insignificant, pause often to let the Lord remind you that you were created in God's image as a totally unique being, and that you're dearly loved by God.

Be alert to Scriptures on this subject that you would like to memorize and frequently meditate on.

GOD'S LOVE THROUGH Christ also shows that *I'm sought after by God.* He says to each of us who will listen, "I have loved you with an everlasting love; therefore with lovingkindness I have drawn you" (Jeremiah 31:3, NKJV).

The Lord's active seeking for us and drawing us near to Himself never ceases: "For the eyes of the LORD move to and fro throughout the earth that He may strongly support those whose heart is completely His" (2 Chronicles 16:9, NASB).

Through our salvation in Christ, we also discover that we have *been created for a high calling and for highly important purposes.* There's an eternal reason for our existence, a reason that is extremely important to God the Father and His Son. Referring to Christ, Paul tells us, "All things were created through Him and *for* Him" (Colossians 1:16, NKJV, emphasis mine). It's in Christ that we're able to fulfill God's words about us in Isaiah 43:6–7, where He speaks of "my sons…and my daughters," and of "everyone who is called by my name, whom I created *for my glory,* whom I formed and made" (NIV, emphasis mine). The wise King Solomon tells us, "The LORD has made all *for Himself*" (Proverbs 16:4, NKJV, emphasis mine). Our reason for living is wrapped up in the loving heart of our mighty God.

Our discovery and experience of this high calling is inseparably linked with our relationship with Jesus Christ—a relationship designed by God Himself, for "he is the one who invited you into this wonderful friendship with his Son, Jesus Christ our Lord" (1 Corinthians 1:9, NLT).

"You are made like God so that God and you can work together in the world He has made.... God and you together can bring into visibility the love, wisdom, and truth of God."

DR. MAURICE WAGNER

As you see and understand it, in what ways can you and God "work together" during the rest of your lifetime here on earth?

A Self-Opinion

Loving Father, You give me so many reasons for deep gratitude
and appreciation for who I really am!

Thank You that I'm Your special creation—unique and wonderful,
personally designed by You and skillfully put together.

Thank You for the high honor and exalted responsibility that You've
given to the entire human race.
And thank You for making me a member of it.

Thank You for sharing something of Yourself by creating us in
Your image. I'm grateful for the sense of high calling and
exalted purpose that these truths give to me.

Most of all, I thank You for demonstrating Your love through Jesus,
my beloved Savior. How grateful I am for all that He said and all
that He accomplished by living on earth and dying and rising from
the dead. I praise and worship You for loving me so deeply and
seeking me and making me Your child.

"To hate ourselves is to despise one whom God loves; it is as much a sin as hating another person…. The only reason we reject ourselves is because we do not feel 'acceptable.' Yet God accepts us, and if the infinite God can accept us, we can learn to accept and love ourselves."

CECIL OSBORNE, *THE ART OF UNDERSTANDING YOURSELF*

What additional evidence of God's exciting love and acceptance can you find and enjoy in the following passages? Feast your soul on these truths!
Psalm 36:7;
Luke 19:10;
Romans 8:1, 32;
Ephesians 3:16–19;
1 John 4:9–10

Too Low

reaLity's negative side 12

As we look at the Scriptures objectively, we can't escape seeing that God has revealed a number of negative realities about us. We can think of these facts as who we are "in the flesh"—that is, in our natural self, independent of God.

Before you and I received Christ, we lived on our own, by our own powers, according to our own desires. Ingrained within us, in our bodies and our personalities, were a multitude of self-centered, self-seeking, self-honoring, self-gratifying patterns of living. The apostle Paul speaks of these patterns as "the flesh" and "sinful flesh" and "sin that dwells in me." It's the part of us that was and is spiritually dead. In various translations of God's Word, it's referred to as our "sinful nature" or the part of us that is "carnal," "worldly," "fleshly," and "unspiritual."

The Bible is clear that this part of us is defiled, disobedient, deceived, empty, purposeless, enslaved, self-willed, defensive, and proud. And it always tries to ignore the one true God.

What have been the most recent ways your sinful nature has displayed itself?

> "God created people to be upright, but they have each turned to follow their own downward path."
>
> ECCLESIASTES 7:29, NLT

WE'RE TO ADMIT that this corrupt part of us exists and that it is unrighteous, just as Paul did: "I know that nothing good dwells in me, that is, in my flesh" (Romans 7:18).

Although as believers in Christ we now share in our innermost being the nature and righteousness of Christ, sin has not yet been eradicated from our personalities. It's still present in our flesh, and it doesn't lose its ugliness as we grow spiritually. In spite of all the grace, insight, and power we enjoy in Christ, we still operate "in the flesh" if we stop relying on Christ or start believing that our way is better than His.

But we're also to remember that this sinful nature is now only our *false* self; it's no longer the "real me"! It's our former self parading as our true self and professing to have our best interests at heart. Our true self is the new person we are in Christ—united with Him, alive with His life, given a position of favor with the living God—cleansed, enriched, and enabled to please and glorify our risen Lord. Having been born of God, we have both a new nature and a new heredity.

We're also to remember that, through Christ's death, the sinful side of us has lost its enslaving hold over us: "Our old sinful selves were crucified with Christ so that sin might lose its power in our lives. We are no longer slaves to sin" (Romans 6:6, NLT).

> "Surely there is not a righteous man on earth who does good and never sins."
> ECCLESIASTES 7:20, ESV

In what ways, if any, is it difficult for you to admit that your sinful nature—and everyone else's—is as ugly as ever? How easy is it for you to say with Paul, "I know that nothing good dwells in my flesh"?

TRULY UNDERSTANDING and acknowledging what we're like in the flesh can humble us, and thus open us to the inflow of God's enabling grace.

But many Christians live constantly in the flesh, never growing spiritually. Others revert to life in the flesh for hours or days or months at a time.

After you became a Christian, have there been periods in your life when you consciously chose to live "in the flesh" instead of endeavoring to obey Christ? If so, what was that experience like for you?

When we choose to live in the flesh for any length of time, we severely block our spiritual growth. To various degrees we continue to base our sense of identity on our natural human qualities rather than on God. We depend on human approval, connections, and status rather than on God's approval and the privileges, status, and endowments He freely grants us. We live our lives not according to God's wisdom but according to the wisdom of the world. This wisdom leads us to be self-centered and to exalt not God but ourselves or other people. This often leads to prideful boasting as a fleshly attempt at trying to feel approved and significant.

Another inevitable result of living "in the flesh" is interpersonal conflict with other believers. This problem was rampant among the Christians in Corinth, and Paul challenged them with these words: "While there is jealousy and strife among you, are you not of the flesh and behaving only in a human way?" (1 Corinthians 3:3, ESV).

That's why it's important to understand our sinful nature and have no illusions regarding it.

Reality's Negative

Holy God, I acknowledge before You the sinfulness of my natural self,
my "flesh." I admit to You the same thing Paul admitted to all of us:
In my flesh, nothing good dwells.

This fact isn't pleasant, but I choose to accept it.
Help me to keep on accepting it and to cast off any
remaining illusions that my self-centered sinful nature can
ever be acceptable to You and useful to me.

I also acknowledge before You that I want no part in living by this
sinful nature and being controlled by it.
I recognize the wonderful and exciting truth that my sinful nature is
now merely my false self. My true self is the "new person altogether"
which I am in Christ (2 Corinthians 5:17, Phillips).

Thank You for breaking my bondage to my sinful nature through
the death of Your only Son whom You love so deeply—Jesus Christ
my Savior. Thank You that my sinful self has been crucified with Him.
Let me not for a single day forget this glorious truth,
or fail to be grateful to You for it.

To discover more about the qualities of the flesh—of indwelling sin—study especially Galatians 5:16–26; Romans 7:14–8:2; and 1 Corinthians 3:1–3.

Which fleshly qualities most often intrude into your experience?

Which truth in these Scriptures helps you the most?

WHO I am IN THE fLesH

Why choose darkness rather than light? "With the Lord's authority let me say this: Live no longer as the ungodly do, for they are hopelessly confused. Their closed minds are full of darkness; they are far away from the life of God because they have shut their minds and hardened their hearts against him" (Ephesians 4:17–18, NLT).

"If anyone walks in the night, he stumbles, because the light is not in him" (John 11:10, ESV). Have you noticed in particular ways how dark your sinful nature is with its absence of God's light?

IT'S BECAUSE OF God's perfect love for us that He makes the truth about our sinful nature so clear in His Word.

He lets us know that He will never improve or remake our "old self," our "flesh." Instead He declares it dead, separated from Him, and He treats it as such. He has no dealings with it—and He asks us to do the same.

The Bible gives a clear and detailed picture of the qualities that belong to our sinful nature. Recognizing these harmful and unbecoming hangovers from our old condition makes us better able to "fling off the dirty clothes of the old way of living, which were rotted through and through with lust's illusions." Then we can "put on the clean fresh clothes of the new life which was made by God's design" (Ephesians 4:22–24, Phillips).

Deliberately seeking to understand what we're like in our natural self can humble us. It can also show us specific ways in which we need God and the positive truths He has given.

The darkness of our sinful nature is dispelled from our personality not by trying to push it out, but simply by letting in light—God's faithful and powerful light.

ONE PLACE IN the Scriptures where we can face the stark reality of our sinful nature—our former nature—is the book of Ephesians. This book abundantly describes the incomparable riches that are ours "in Christ," and it also abounds with true pictures of what we are like "in the flesh."

Paul directly links our "old self"—our sinful nature—with what we were like before we became Christians. He emphasizes Christ's instruction to "put off *your old self,* which *belongs to your former manner of life*" (Ephesians 4:22, ESV).

The reality of our former nature, Paul says, is that it is "rotten through and through, full of lust and deception" (Ephesians 4:22, NLT). It is marked by "following the course and fashion of this world," by "obeying Satan, the mighty prince of the power of the air," and by "indulging the desires of the flesh and of the mind" (Ephesians 2:2, AMP and NLT; 2:3, NASB).

Keep in mind that the "old self" includes our hidden potential for evil. This varies from person to person.

It is characterized by a heart that is hopeless, with "nothing to look forward to and no God to whom you could turn" (2:12, Phillips)—and by a mind that is "closed" and "full of darkness" (4:18, NLT).

In many people, it includes being self-righteous

Especially tragic is its alienation. It is "cut off from the life of God through ignorance and insensitiveness" (4:18, Phillips). This separation leads to "spiritual apathy" and "unbridled sensuality" (4:19, AMP).

> The sinful mind is hostile to God. It does not submit to God's law, nor can it do so. Those controlled by the sinful nature cannot please God,
>
> ROMANS 8:7–8, NIV

TWICE IN THE PSALMS, David reminds us that "God looks down from heaven" on all mankind and observes that every one of us is "corrupt" (14:1–3; 53:1–3, ESV). In our natural flesh, not a single one of us has a consistent inclination either to do good or to seek after God. Instead, our flesh is fully prone toward "doing evil deeds" (Colossians 1:21, ESV), and is persistently God's enemy. "The sinful nature is always hostile to God" (Romans 8:7, NLT).

Consider our Lord's liberating promise to His people in Ezekiel 11:19 (KJV): "I will put a new spirit within you." What are the assumptions behind such a promise?

That's a glimpse of the unpleasant truth about our flesh which the Scriptures expose again and again. But we're not to stop there. We're not to dwell there or live there, for we're in danger if we identify too much with our "old self." The more we see ourselves that way, the more our old fleshly patterns of life take over.

He did that when we were born again.

Our old nature is enslaved to death and darkness, and we should harbor no illusions that it can ever be reformed. But God invites us to see ourselves as altogether new persons. "The old has passed away; behold, the new has come" (2 Corinthians 5:17, ESV). We're to fully identify with the new person we are in Christ—with our new heredity and life, with our new position and privileges, with our new resources, our new responsibilities, our new possibilities.

Throughout the rest of this book, we want to richly explore what this newness can mean for our sense of identity—for a true realization of who we are in Christ.

Who I Am in

❧

*Thank You, Lord, that I can face the existence of my sinful nature with
the breathtaking knowledge that I am a new person in Christ Jesus.
I leave the old behind and run forward, eager to enjoy all the newness
and fullness You have for me!*

*Out of my bondage, sorrow, and night,
Jesus, I come, Jesus, I come;
Into Thy freedom, gladness, and light,
Jesus, I come to Thee;
Out of my sickness, into Thy health,
Out of my want and into Thy wealth,
Out of my sin and into Thyself,
Jesus, I come to Thee.*

How would you summarize the most important things you've learned about your "flesh," your sinful nature?

*Out of my shameful failure and loss,
Jesus, I come, Jesus, I come;
Into the glorious gain of Thy cross,
Jesus, I come to Thee.
Out of earth's sorrows into Thy balm,
Out of life's storms and into Thy calm,
Out of distress to jubilant psalm,
Jesus, I come to Thee.* *

* Words by William T. Sleeper, 1887

the Flesh

YOUR Life
IS
CHRIST

CONTINUING the adventure

14

AGAINST THE DARK backdrop of the negative facts about us—what we're like in our sinful flesh—God paints a beautiful portrait of who we are *in Christ*. He reveals amazing and glorious truths of who we are *in Christ*—about what we are like in the realm that matters most both now and forever. Our oneness with Christ provides the ultimate, totally reliable supports that each of us needs for our sense of identity. The secret lies in who the Lord is and who we see ourselves to be.

As we hear and believe all that God tells us—as we intentionally think these truths and begin to act accordingly—He liberates us and unfolds the true personality He designed us to be.

In the rest of this book we'll look at passages that unveil truths which God has used to liberate many. I often go back to these Scriptures to deepen my understanding of who He says I am. Repeatedly He reminds me to depend more constantly on the incredible oneness I have with Christ. I pray that He will do the same for you.

"If the Holy Spirit controls your mind, there is life and peace" (Romans 8:6, NLT). Even at this very moment, what can you do by decisive choice to give the Spirit of God more control over your sense of identity?

As we feast on these rich truths about who we are in Christ, we're able to renovate our inner identity album, making it realistic and uplifting.

At first our inner album is mainly about the psychological and social side of us. But as we let God lovingly invade our lives through our faith in Christ, He provides what is essentially a new album. This album covers the most distinctly human part of us—our spirit, which came to life when we accepted God's gift of salvation through Christ. As we relate to God as our Father, He fills our new album with images that give unshakable support for our sense of identity. He also develops in us a new love and competence in relating to other people. This means that the psychological part of us receives increased support through our human relationships.

So we no longer need to find our identity through our appearance, performance, and status.

We learn to think of our physical *appearance* as simply a "picture frame" in which we can display God's love and sufficiency.

Our *performance* becomes simply an *expression* of who we really are in Christ, rather than an attempt to gain support for our self image.

And our *status* is important only as it gives us opportunity to glorify God and serve others. It does not indicate who we are!

Our actions become a way of giving love rather than trying to earn an ego-building response from other people. We no longer need to depend on how people respond to us, and we escape from evaluating ourselves in the mirror of human approval.

In what ways have you tried to find your identity through your appearance, performance, or status? Think carefully about this. If you recognize ways that you've been depending on these things, openly acknowledge this to God and release these areas into His loving hands.

As you continue your adventure of exploring the vast array of truths about who you are in Christ, keep in mind that many of these are true whether or not we know about them or are consciously experiencing them. Others are *potentially* true. Their reality for us depends on our responses to the Lord. Do we trust Him? Do we yield to Him and rely on Him to forgive us when we sin and to transform us?

Another crucial concept to keep in mind is that every truth about us is rooted in who *God* is—His attributes, attitudes, and actions. For example, because He is love, we are loved. Because He's the Redeemer who shed His blood for us, we are ransomed from sin's guilt and condemnation. Because He's the Giver, we can be receivers. Because He desires us, we are both desirable and desired. Because He has chosen us, we are intimately related to the Supreme Ruler of all. The portrait God has revealed of Himself undergirds His portrait of who we are in Christ.

This also means that for every need or problem we face, there's always a corresponding truth (or truths) about *Him* that can see us through triumphantly, with calm trust in Him.

To keep learning more about Him, we keep returning to our most complete revelation of Him: His written Word. Everything the Scriptures record reveals Him—the commandments, history, poetry, prophecy, promises. All reveals His personality, His ways, His standards and plans and gracious purposes, and His heart for each of us.

"Revive and stimulate me according to Your word!" (Psalm 119:25 AMP). In your own words, ask God to show you Himself, that you may better understand yourself.

Continuing the

*Father, I'm so glad for the beautiful portrait in Your
Word of who I am in Christ. Thank You for revealing these truths—
truths which we humans so desperately need.*

*I celebrate the fact that I never again need to rely on my appearance,
my performance or my status to define who I am.
I invite You to lovingly invade all my thinking about myself.
Expose further ways in which I'm holding on to what is deceptive
and inadequate, and encourage me to cling to the exciting truths You
have revealed—truths that confirm who I really am in Your sight.*

*I praise You for how faithful You are to enlighten me, to deliver me,
and to support me. Thank You for teaching me to yield more fully to
You and obey You more constantly. Guide me in the adventure of full
reliance on You. I trust You to transform me and empower me,
enabling me to fulfill all You have in mind for me to be and do.*

Reflect fully on Isaiah
55:8–13. According to
this passage, what does
the Word of God
accomplish in the lives
of His people?

Adventure

knowing my need

A DIAMOND IS DISPLAYED most dramatically against black velvet. Even so, the positive facts about who we are in Christ are always most striking when we remember the dark backdrop of what we were like before we received Christ. We were spiritually dead, defiled, disobedient, and deceived. We ignored God and lived in darkness—empty, enslaved, self-willed, and having no worthy purpose for living.

At this time in your life, what most qualifies you to receive God's help?

The glorious truths of who we are in Christ shine with increasing brightness as we honestly acknowledge our deep need for God and cast away our self-centered pride. The Scriptures make it clear that we qualify for God's working when we admit that we are poor, needy, weak, and dependent.

Through the Scriptures, as well as through our daily problems and failures, God reveals to us our sins, our limitations, and our immeasurable need for Him. We need this humbling view of ourselves. It prevents us from taking credit for our positive qualities and achievements, from feeling self-sufficient or superior to other persons, and from being content with our status quo.

TO HELP US UNDERSTAND how perfectly God provides for us, He lets us hunger psychologically or emotionally or spiritually, then meets that heightened need with Himself. In a similar way He allowed the people of Israel to hunger physically after He brought them out of Egypt, then fed them with manna from heaven. Moses later reminded them that God did this "to teach you that people need more than bread for their life; real life comes by feeding on every word of the LORD" (Deuteronomy 8:3, NLT). That's a lesson regarding our own needs as well!

God keeps assuring us of His intention to help the needy: "For the LORD hears the needy and does not despise his own people" (Psalm 69:33, ESV). "He stands beside the needy, ready to save them" (Psalm 109:31, NLT). "God blesses those who realize their need for him, for the Kingdom of Heaven is given to them" (Matthew 5:3, NLT).

So whenever your longing for meaning or belongingness or significance (or whatever) is like an intense thirst, find help in remembering what God is like: "When the poor and needy seek water, and there is none, and their tongue is parched with thirst, I the LORD will answer them; I the God of Israel will not forsake them. I will open rivers on the bare heights, and fountains in the midst of the valleys. I will make the wilderness a pool of water, and the dry land springs of water" (Isaiah 41:17–18, ESV).

"And you must remember how the Eternal your God led you through the desert...to teach you your need of Him."

DEUTERONOMY 8:2, MOFFATT

In what ways has God been faithful in allowing you to "hunger" and "thirst" for a more reliable and positive sense of identity?

As we recognize what God is like, we can freely admit how needy we are. We can acknowledge with David, "I am poor and needy, and my heart is wounded within me" (Psalm 109:22, NIV). In our shortcomings we can know the same truth David knew: "As for me, I am poor and needy, but *the Lord is thinking about me right now*" (Psalm 40:17, NLT, emphasis mine). Talk about significance! The King of kings is thinking about us!

So we can ask Him earnestly, with confidence, "Do not withhold Your tender mercies from me, O LORD; let Your lovingkindness and Your truth continually preserve me.... O LORD, make haste to help me!" (Psalm 40:11, 13, NKJV).

As we see with greater clarity the truth about ourselves, the Lord enables us to tell Him even this: "I desire you more than anything on earth" (Psalm 73:25, NLT). And: "I have Thee as my very own in the land of the living" (Psalm 142:5, Moffatt). This in no way excludes love for humans, but it elevates God to first place in our hearts and lives.

The more we see God responding to our needs, the more we'll be able to affirm with David, "My soul finds rest in God alone; my salvation comes from him. He alone is my rock and my salvation; he is my fortress, I will never be shaken" (Psalm 62:1–2, NIV).

> The humble will be filled with fresh joy from the LORD.
> Those who are poor will rejoice in the Holy One of Israel.
>
> ISAIAH 29:19, NLT

To what degree are you able to honestly tell God right now, as the psalmist did, "I desire You more than anything on earth" and "I have You as my very own in the land of the living"? As you recognize any shortcoming in your love for God, freely express your deficiency to Him, with confidence in His forgiveness, His understanding, His love for you, and His power to deepen your love for Him.

Knowing My Need

~~~

I'm so grateful, Lord, that I don't have to try to hide my needs.
I can always openly confess them before You,
as part of my ongoing relationship with You.

I thank You that You meet me where I am and that You are
at work in me to make me more than I am.
So I choose to thank You for Your gracious attitude toward the
ways I fall short. What a comfort to know that You fully
understand the feeling of my weaknesses and inadequacies.

In the following specific ways, I acknowledge that I am
poor, needy, weak, and dependent:

Think about how fully and genuinely you can identify with the needs experienced in the following Scripture passages:
Psalms 31:3; 34:6; 54:4; 69:29; 70:5; 86:1–2; 109:22;
Hebrews 13:6

Which passages *most* help you to acknowledge:
a. what your needs are;
b. what you can count on God to be to you and do for you.

caLLeD aND cHoseN

16

YOU ARE *CALLED.* You've been called personally *by* God and *to* God. That's an in-Christ fact about you that can help erase any sense of alienation or lack of purpose that you may at times feel.

We know that this calling is personal because God uses our name. To each of His people He says, "I have called you by your name; you are Mine" (Isaiah 43:1, NKJV). Jesus taught that a good shepherd "calls his own sheep by name" (John 10:3, NKJV). And of course Christ Himself is that Good Shepherd whose voice we can sense in our hearts, speaking our name.

Our calling is actually older than we are. In His Word, God teaches each of His servants to acknowledge this: "The LORD called me from the womb, from the body of my mother he named my name" (Isaiah 49:1, ESV). We can hear from the Lord the same assurance He gave the prophet Jeremiah: "Before I formed you in the womb I knew you" (Jeremiah 1:5, NKJV).

In this world of noise and hurry, learn to daily get away and turn to God to hear His voice: "Truly my soul silently waits for God" (Psalm 62:1, NKJV).

WE ARE "called according to his purpose" (Romans 8:28, ESV), and that purpose includes not only effective service for God but also an intimate relationship with Him. The Lord tells His people, "I have called you...so you can serve me" (Isaiah 41:9, NLT). And we're "called into the companionship of His Son, our Lord Jesus Christ" (1 Corinthians 1:9, Berkeley).

Everything about His calling of us is permeated with His own eternal and changeless character. He "called us with a holy calling...according to His own purpose and grace which was given to us in Christ Jesus before time began" (2 Timothy 1:9, NKJV).

Behind this calling is God's own active *choice*. We are called by Him because we have been *chosen* by Him.

His choice of us exalts us to a status of worth beyond compare. This is true of all who believe in Him and belong to Him: "The LORD your God has chosen you...to be His valued possession" (Deuteronomy 7:6, Berkeley). We're all "the people whom he has chosen as his heritage" (Psalm 33:12, ESV).

His reason for choosing us flows out of His loving character and His faithfulness to fulfill His promises. "The LORD fastened His affection upon you and chose you...because the LORD loved you, and on account of His oath which He had sworn" (Deuteronomy 7:6–8, Berkeley).

> "How blessed is the one whom You choose and bring near to You."
>
> PSALM 65:4, NASB

TO BE CHOSEN is the opposite of being rejected. God says, "You are My servant," and He reminds each of us, "I have chosen you and not rejected you" (Isaiah 41:9, NASB). As believers in Christ, we never need to fear God's rejection.

As with everything else in God's actions and attitudes toward us, His choice of us is inseparably linked with His eternal love: "Long ago, even before he made the world, God loved us and chose us in Christ to be holy and without fault in his eyes" (Ephesians 1:4, NLT). This everlasting and decisive love is wrapped up with His sovereign will: "He chose us from the beginning, and all things happen just as he decided long ago" (Ephesians 1:11, NLT).

Do you to any extent fear that God will reject you? If so, talk with Him about this.

Our eternal calling stretches as far into the future as it does into the past, and it ensures our share in the Lord's glory. "And those whom he predestined he also called, and those whom he called he also justified, and those whom he justified he also glorified" (Romans 8:30, ESV).

How should we respond to this surpassingly rich truth that we have been called by God? He lets us know: "Lead a life worthy of your calling, for you have been called by God" (Ephesians 4:1, NLT). "Just as he who called you is holy, so be holy in all you do" (1 Peter 1:15, NIV).

Called and Chosen

My heart rejoices in You, Lord, for the amazing privilege of being chosen by You in eternity past and being called by You with a holy calling. How wonderful to know that I never need to fear that You will reject me.

I celebrate the fact that I've been called according to Your purpose, and that Your purpose includes both intimate relationship with You and effective service for You. I'm part of Your chosen family— set apart to be Your treasured possession!

And thank You for making Your Son my Good Shepherd who calls me by name.

And Lord, I count on You to guide and empower me to lead a life worthy of my holy calling.

Thank You again that I'm a chosen one—called to love and obey the King of kings and Lord of lords, the Supreme Ruler of all things.

Look up the following passages to find out more about your being called and choosen by God. As you explore these Scriptures, ask the Lord to increase two things—your faith in what He says about you, and your moment-by-moment obedience. Colossians 3:12; 2 Timothy 2:19; 2 Thessalonians 2:13–15; Titus 1:1; 3:14; Philippians 1:27; 2:13–15

Desired

GOD'S CHOICE of us arose out of the fervent passion of His heart. He called and chose us because He *desires* us.

He uses the picture of a king and his bride to show us this truth. As the Sovereign One, He makes sure His royal bride hears how much she means to Him: "The king is enthralled by your beauty" (Psalm 45:11, NIV).

This portrait of royal desire is continued with great intensity throughout the Song of Solomon. In the song's words we can hear the Kingly One describe His love for us. We can rejoice as He says, "Rise up, my love, my fair one, and come away.... O my dove... let me see your face, let me hear your voice; for your voice is sweet, and your face is lovely" (Song of Solomon 2:10–14, NKJV).

We can therefore joyfully answer, "I am my beloved's, and his desire is for me" (Song of Solomon 7:10, NASB).

Allow the Lord to fully convince your heart that He desires you. What is your understanding of the basis and the reason for His desire?

AS WE FREELY approach this One who desires us so intensely, our response triggers "joy in the presence of the angels of God" (Luke 15:10, NKJV). For we were lost, but now we're found—just like the missing coin and the stray lamb and the wayward son in the stories Jesus told in Luke 15. We're the returning prodigal swept up in a parent's passionate welcome: "But while he was still a long way off, his father saw him and felt compassion, and ran and embraced him and kissed him" (Luke 15:20, ESV).

Though we're "prone to wander," as the old hymn says, the Lord's desire ensures His active courtship of us as His bride: "I will allure her," He says, "put her alone and apart, and speak to her heart" (Hosea 2:14, Moffatt).

In His prayer on the night before He was crucified, Jesus expressed His relentless desire for us. Using words about our future that are breathtaking for us to hear, He said, "Father, I want those you have given me to be with me where I am, and to see my glory" (John 17:24, NIV).

The Lord of heaven and earth loves to bestow rich gifts on His desired ones. Therefore we can confidently look forward to seeing and experiencing "all that God has prepared (made and keeps ready) for those who love Him" (1 Corinthians 2:9, AMP).

The future is as bright as the love and promises of our Most Beloved One.

Have you been spiritually aware of God expressing His desire for you? In what ways have you sensed His seeking to allure your heart? How have you sensed the Lord's embrace?

THE LORD'S DESIRE for us means we'll never be separated from His loving notice and His concern for us. We can exclaim, as our brother David did, "Look how the Eternal marks me out for favor! The Eternal listens when I call to Him" (Psalm 4:3, Moffatt). And we can join David as he cries out with delight, "How precious are your thoughts about me, O God! They are innumerable! I can't even count them; they outnumber the grains of sand!" (Psalm 139:17–18, NLT).

> "The eye of the LORD is on those who fear Him, on those who hope in His mercy" (Psalm 33:18, NKJV). When you think of His eye upon you, what emotion does that bring to you?

This God of boundless love sees and knows everything about us. As we rest in the righteousness of Christ, we can count on His loving attention: "The eyes of the LORD are on the righteous" (Psalm 34:15, NKJV).

He who numbers the very hairs of our head cannot forget us, for He says, "See, I have engraved you on the palms of my hands" (Matthew 10:30; Isaiah 49:16, NIV).

We can therefore let go of our insecurities, for our God is a God of kind intention, with good purposes and special plans for each and all of His loved ones. He declares in Jeremiah 29:11, ESV, "For I know the plans I have for you...plans for wholeness and not for evil." We are "planned for" in love, never left to roam or drift or fend for ourselves. We can praise God as David did: "Your plans for us are too numerous to list" (Psalm 40:5, NLT).

Desired

I love You, Lord, because You have first loved me (1 John 4:10).
You are my Beloved and I am Yours, and I rejoice that
Your desire is for me. You have made me a new person
in Christ, whom You delight in.

I rejoice that Your desire for me never turns cold, but that
You continue to shower me with Your gifts and blessings.
You are always thinking of me, providing for me, guiding me.

And thank You for running to me in my need and
putting Your loving arms around me.

For all this and more, I offer You my praise
and thanksgiving—and my love!

In John 17:20–26, review the things Jesus prayed for us just before He was betrayed and crucified. What do these words reveal about the intensity and nature of His desire for us?

No Longer Condemned

"When we were God's
enemies, we were
reconciled to him
through the death
of his Son."

Romans 5:10, NIV

What makes you most
grateful for your new
guilt-free identity
in Christ?

In my old identity—my former self—guilt persisted as a prominent feature. My guilt was like a strong glue that bonded me to sin and death. Even when I got faint glimpses of the fact that sin was my enemy and that I was enslaved to it, guilt held me like a vice under sin's rule. The law saw to that. It held me to the penalty I had brought on myself by aligning myself with sin.

I stood condemned before God because I was a fallen person—contaminated by sin, unfit for intimacy with the Holy One. I had erected barricades against Him, choosing to go my own way.

In this regard I was like every other human being, just as the apostle Paul says: "We ourselves were thoughtless, disobedient, led astray, slaves to passions and pleasures of all sorts, wasting our time in malice and envy, detestable, and hating one another" (Titus 3:3, Berkeley).

But now I have a guilt-free identity in Christ for one reason alone: "The goodness and loving kindness of God our Savior appeared" (Titus 3:4, ESV).

Now in Christ I can continually savor the fact that through His sacrifice, I can joyfully view myself as acquitted. I'm no longer condemned!

What greater relief and joy can there be for one whose guilt was so real? "Blessed and happy and to be envied are those whose iniquities are forgiven and whose sins are covered up and completely buried. Blessed and happy and to be envied is the person of whose sin the Lord will take no account nor reckon it against him" (Romans 4:7–8, AMP).

"So then there is no condemnation at all for those who are in union with Christ Jesus" (Romans 8:1, Williams). Such condemnation no longer exists. The reason for it is gone, by virtue of what Christ's death achieved: "God crossed out the whole debt against us in His account books. He no longer counted the laws that we had broken. He nailed the account book to the cross and closed the account" (Colossians 2:14, Laubach).

What convinces you that your guilt before God was real, and required the death of Christ for your atonement?

Therefore "we have an Advocate with the Father, Jesus Christ the righteous; and He Himself is the propitiation for our sins" (1 John 2:1–2, NASB). He is the atoning sacrifice, the personal atonement! (Williams; Phillips).

From the lips of the Lord Jesus comes this firm promise: "I most solemnly say to you, whoever listens to me and believes Him who has sent me...will never come under condemnation" (John 5:24, Williams). With joy we hear the Lord's good news: "Do not be afraid, for I have ransomed you" (Isaiah 43:1, NLT).

THINK CAREFULLY about the meaning in these uplifting words from Paul: "Who would dare to accuse us, whom God has chosen? The judge himself has declared us free from sin. Who is in a position to condemn? Only Christ, and Christ died for us, Christ rose for us, Christ reigns in power for us, Christ prays for us!" (Romans 8:33–34, Phillips).

Considering what our sin cost our Lord Jesus, He could rightfully be our accuser. Instead He reigns for us and intercedes for us and actively supports us in our righteous living.

So we escape the penalty we've earned. "He has not punished us for all our sins, nor does he deal with us as we deserve" (Psalm 103:10, NLT). The next verse displays the reason for this mercy from God's hands—His marvelous, boundless love! "For as high as the heavens are above the earth, so great is his steadfast love toward those who fear him" (Psalm 103:11, ESV).

The LORD redeems the soul of His servants, and none of those who trust in Him shall be condemned.

PSALM 34:22, NKJV

"My rescue comes from Him alone; rock, rescue, refuge, He is all to me."

PSALM 62:1–2, MOFFATT

Take time to come before the Lord with careful reflection on what He has done to liberate you from condemnation, and what He continues to do to enrich your freedom. What do you wish to say to Him about this?

No Longer

Lord God, You are mighty to save! (Isaiah 63:1).

Thank You for delivering me from the condemnation I deserve, and for overcoming the barricades I had erected in my heart against You.

In God's presence, treasure your freedom from condemnation by reflecting on the following passages: Isaiah 54:17; John 3:17–18; Galatians 3:13

How grateful I am for the guilt-free identity that is mine in Your Son, Jesus Christ, the Holy One. Thank You that You "made Him who knew no sin to be sin on our behalf, so that we might become the righteousness of God in Him" (2 Corinthians 5:21, NASB). He ransomed me for You, and now I'm fully Yours.

Thank You that Jesus is my advocate, my merciful and faithful High Priest before You, who comes to my aid when I am tempted, providing the way of escape (Hebrews 8:1; 2:17–18; 1 Corinthians 10:13).

And thank You again that in Christ I'm no longer condemned. Help me remember to thank You for this regularly, daily, as long as I live. "For you love me so much! You are constantly so kind! You have rescued me from deepest hell" (Psalm 86:13, TLB).

cLean anD more

WE CAN THINK of our redemption in so many wonderful ways.

It means being *clean*. Jesus tells His followers, "You are clean," and again, "Already you are clean" (John 13:10; 15:3, ESV). The cleansing goes deep, for the blood of Christ is able to "purify our souls from the deeds of death, that we may serve the living God" (Hebrews 9:14, Phillips).

Ages ago, when God through His prophets promised His people a new covenant, He let them know that it would mean complete purification: "You will be clean; I will cleanse you from all your impurities and from all your idols.... I will save you from all your uncleanness" (Ezekiel 36:25, 29, NIV).

So He has said to us, "No matter how deep the stain of your sins, I can remove it. I can make you as clean as freshly fallen snow. Even if you are stained as red as crimson, I can make you as white as wool" (Isaiah 1:18, NLT).

> "He has removed our rebellious acts as far away from us as the east is from the west."
>
> PSALM 103:12, NLT

WE ARE CLEAN because our sins have been washed away (1 Corinthians 6:11, NLT). Our forgiveness has been purchased at the highest price possible, so it is precious beyond imagining: "In Him we have redemption *through His blood*, the forgiveness of sins" (Ephesians 1:7, NKJV).

God forgives us not simply for our sake, but also for His sake: "I, I am he who blots out your transgressions for my own sake" (Isaiah 43:25, ESV). In forgiving and removing our sins, He is fulfilling His ancient promise to His people: "I will forgive their iniquity, and their sin I will remember no more" (Jeremiah 31:34, NKJV).

God's forgiveness flows from the essence of His character, so we can say with David, "O Lord, you are so good, so ready to forgive, so full of unfailing love for all who ask your aid" (Psalm 86:5, NLT).

So He encourages us to quickly and sincerely acknowledge our offenses. "If we confess our sins, He is to be depended on, since He is just, to forgive us our sins and to cleanse us from every wrong" (1 John 1:9, Williams). We can count on God to be like the prodigal son's father—not giving us an additional lecture when we come in repentance, but calling for a robe and a ring and a feast in our honor! (Luke 15:17–24).

Open yourself to the Holy Spirit's counsel and conviction. Are there any offenses against the Lord which you should acknowledge at this time, in view of all He has gone through for you?

OUR REDEMPTION does not merely mean that we're no longer "wrong" in God's eyes. It also means that we are fully "made right with God through Christ" (2 Corinthians 5:21, NLT). "We are justified (acquitted, declared righteous, and given a right standing with God) through faith" (Romans 5:1, AMP).

Being redeemed means not only casting off the ragged, soiled clothing of our sins, but also putting on glorious new garments of righteousness. So we can exclaim, "I will greatly rejoice in the LORD; my soul shall exult in my God, for he has clothed me with the garments of salvation; he has covered me with the robe of righteousness, as a bridegroom decks himself like a priest with a beautiful headdress, and as a bride adorns herself with her jewels" (Isaiah 61:10, ESV).

This verse is a beautiful picture of what it means to be "justified freely by his grace through the redemption that came by Christ Jesus" (Romans 3:24, NIV).

All of this calls for our grateful response, in how we live and how we approach God: "Since we have these promises, dear friends, let us purify ourselves from everything that contaminates body and spirit" (2 Corinthians 7:1, NIV). We can acknowledge as the psalmist did, "There is forgiveness with You...that You may be reverently feared and worshiped" (Psalm 130:4, AMP).

> You have been made right with God because of what the Lord Jesus Christ and the Spirit of our God have done for you.
>
> 1 CORINTHIANS 6:11, NLT

The Lord asks us to purify ourselves from anything that contaminates body or spirit. To accomplish this, is there any action you should be taking at this time?

Clean and More

Thank You, Father, that I'm no longer defiled and corrupt!
In Christ I'm entirely clean—and through His blood I can "escape the
corruption in the world caused by evil desires" (2 Peter 1:4, NIV).
You have purified my conscience from its deadly defilement.
How I thank You!

Now, Lord, with all Your redeemed people I have the privilege of
drawing near to You "with a sincere heart in full assurance of faith,
having my heart sprinkled to cleanse me from a guilty conscience and
having my body washed with pure water"
(Hebrews 10:22, NIV, personalized).

How I thank You that I have been bathed by my
new birth—and now I only have to wash my feet by
simply confessing when I fail to obey You.

I draw near to You this very moment to celebrate the ever-refreshing
cleanness You have given me in my inmost being.
I come to You wearing the clean and shining robe of righteousness,
the garments of salvation which You have clothed me with.

Thank You again that as a new person in Christ I am forever clean.

"I have swept away your offenses like a cloud, your sins like the morning mist. Return to me, for I have redeemed you."
ISAIAH 44:22, NIV

"Let the people turn from their wicked deeds. Let them banish from their minds the very thought of doing wrong! Let them turn to the LORD that he may have mercy on them. Yes, turn to our God, for he will abundantly pardon."
ISAIAH 55:7, NLT

Are there ways at this time that you need to more fully turn to the Lord to experience His forgiveness and His indwelling sufficiency?

aLive with his Life

AT OUR NEW BIRTH, such a radical, night-and-day change took place in our innermost being—in our true and eternal person—that the Bible refers to it as passing out of death into life. "And you He made alive, who were dead in trespasses and sins" (Ephesians 2:1, NKJV).

> "Look upon yourselves as…alive and sensitive to the call of God through Jesus Christ our Lord."
> ROMANS 6:11, PHILLIPS

Our entrance into this spiritual aliveness is inseparably linked with Christ's resurrection. "God is so rich in mercy, and he loved us so very much, that even while we were dead because of our sins, he gave us life when he raised Christ from the dead" (Ephesians 2:4–5, NLT).

> As one author put it, "It's not only true that our life is Christ's, but our life is Christ."

Therefore we can now view ourselves as "alive to God, alert to him, through Jesus Christ our Lord" (Romans 6:11, TLB). "For by the death He died He once for all ended His relation to sin, so you too must consider yourselves as having ended your relation to sin but living in unbroken relation to God through union with Christ Jesus" (Romans 6:10–11, Williams). And in a way that was utterly impossible before, we have become "alive to all that is good" (1 Peter 2:24, Phillips).

THIS GOD with whom you now have unbroken access and relationship is "the life-giving God" (1 Timothy 6:13, Message).

We learn from Jesus how to continually esteem God the Father as the constant source of life. Jesus called Him "the living Father" (John 6:57), and He told us "The Father has life in Himself and is self-existent" (John 5:26, AMP). Therefore "the Father raises the dead and gives them life" (John 5:21, NASB), for "He is not the God of the dead, but of the living" (Luke 20:38, NIV).

Consider what it means personally for you that God "gives life to the dead and calls into existence the things that do not exist" (Romans 4:17, ESV).

Reflect as well on how all your spiritual aliveness is drawn from the life of Christ Himself, "the author of life" (Acts 3:15, NLT). By believing in Jesus, you "have already passed from death into life" (John 5:24, NLT).

> What does it mean for you personally that God "gives life to the dead and calls into existence the things that do not exist" (Romans 4:17, ESV)?

Listen to how Jesus so closely identifies your life with Himself. He says, "I am the resurrection and the life…. Because I live, you will live also…. The Son also gives life to whom He wishes" (John 11:25; 14:19; 5:21, NASB).

Christ has imparted this life to you and to me by the wonderful gift of the Holy Spirit, for "it is the Spirit who gives life" (John 6:63, NASB). He is "the Spirit of life," the One who "makes alive" (Romans 8:2; 2 Corinthians 3:6, AMP).

NOW THAT YOU and I have received "this wildly extravagant life-gift" (Romans 5:17, Message), it's a vital and daily possibility for "the resurrection life of Jesus" to "be shown forth by and in our bodies" (2 Corinthians 4:10, AMP). You and I "may henceforth live to and for God" (Galatians 2:19, AMP), rather than living selfishly.

Our heavenly Father longs for us to experience all that this means. He says, "Give yourselves completely to God since you have been given new life" (Romans 6:13, NLT).

He wants this new aliveness to transform how we think: "Since you have been raised to new life with Christ, set your sights on the realities of heaven, where Christ sits at God's right hand in the place of honor and power" (Colossians 3:1, NLT). "Apply your mind to things above, not to things on earth" (Colossians 3:2, Berkeley).

So we're to keep coming to the Scriptures and nurturing our minds with the truth we find there. Jesus promises, "Whoever continues to feed on Me—whoever takes Me for his food and is nourished by Me—shall in his turn live through and because of Me" (John 6:57, AMP).

Then from personal experience we can offer our Lord and Savior the same profound praise that Peter did: "You have the words of eternal life" (John 6:68).

> "It is He Himself Who gives life."
>
> ACTS 17:25, AMP

> In what ways are you feeling more alive in Christ than ever, as you learn and grow spiritually?

Alive with His Life

I give thanks to You, Father, for giving me life—not only physical life, but also spiritual life! You have made me spiritually alive through the resurrection of Christ, who is my life.

I magnify You for the mighty power You displayed when You raised Your Son from the tomb. What an incredible exhibit of Your life-giving power! How I rejoice that this same life—the life of Christ—is mine. And by it, in my innermost being, I can live in unbroken union with You just as Your Son Jesus does. Thank You, my mighty and loving Father!

And thank You for the gift of Your Holy Spirit, the Spirit of life. How grateful I am for how He sustains me in this new aliveness, as my constant source of spiritual breath and health and wholeness.

Like breathing in fresh air, allow your mind to reflect on the liberating truths found in the following passages— truths about your new aliveness in Christ. John 6:33, 51; 8:12; 14:6; 17:3; 20:30–31; 2 Corinthians 4:11–12; 1 Timothy 6:12

Thank You for connecting me eternally with the realities of heaven, where Christ sits at Your right hand in honor and power. And thank You for awakening my mind and heart so that I can think about these realities, and treasure them, and turn from fleshly ways as I depend on His life in me.

You are the God who "preserves alive all living things" (1 Timothy 6:13, AMP). I acknowledge that all of my life—physical and spiritual— is in Your hands and under Your control.

Thank You again that, through my union with Christ, I'm alive with His life.

21
DEAD TO SIN

OUR NEW LIFE comes hand in hand with a corresponding death.

We share in Christ's resurrection because we share also in His crucifixion and burial. "Our old self was crucified with him so that the body of sin might be done away with, that we should no longer be slaves to sin" (Romans 6:6, NIV). "We were therefore buried with him through baptism into death in order that, just as Christ was raised from the dead through the glory of the Father, we too may live a new life" (Romans 6:4, NIV).

We're to consider ourselves "dead to sin" (Romans 6:11), because "those who belong to Christ Jesus have nailed the passions and desires of their sinful nature to his cross and crucified them there" (Galatians 5:24, NLT). As Laubach translates Colossians 2:14, He nailed the account book to the cross and closed the account.

With Paul we can say, "I have been crucified with Christ" (Galatians 2:20). We can glory in "the cross of our Lord Jesus Christ, by whom the world has been crucified to me, and I to the world" (Galatians 6:14, NKJV).

Pause and take time to worship the Lord today by glorying in the cross of our Lord Jesus Christ. In His presence, reflect on what His death has meant in your relationship to sin.

BEING "DEAD" and "alive"—dead to sin and alive to God—go together. The two truths are inseparable, beautifully designed to function together. We can think about and analyze them separately, but we must keep them together as we count on them and live them out.

We're not to say with gritted teeth and clenched fists, "I'm dead to sin, I'm dead to sin...I insist I'm dead to sin!" Rather we're to gratefully acknowledge, "I'm dead to sin...*and alive to God!* I've died out of the old sinful living. That's no longer the real me. Now I'm alive with His righteous, beautiful life—for time and eternity!" This is now the "real me"! The final focus of our reckoning must always be on the wonderful aliveness God has granted to us.

So we're to continually rely on the facts that we have died to sin *and* we have risen to God. We're dead as far as sin in concerned, crucified through Christ's death...but we're also alive with Christ's powerful life, alive through His resurrection. Together these two truths about us cancel out our old relationship with sin and death and inaugurate our new relationship with God.

We don't make these things true simply by considering them so; it's not a matter of hoodwinking ourselves or creating something through positive thinking. Rather, it's accepting as fact what God says has happened and depending on those facts in our daily life.

God wants us to believe Him—to take Him at His Word. He asks us to consider ourselves to be what we are: dead to sin but alive to God in Christ Jesus.

In this moment, engage your mind to actively count on the facts that you are dead to sin and alive to God. Why are these truths important to understand? Express to the Lord your personal acceptance of these facts, and how much you appreciate their value.

Write down a brief statement of truth to use day by day, hour by hour.

THIS NEW, Christ-centered view of who we are (which is unquestionably true, for God cannot lie) provides the basis for living a righteous, obedient life. The more we see who we are in Christ, the more the idea of flirting with sin becomes inconceivable and utterly out of place.

When sin tries to masquerade as our true being—when it presses its claim on us and pretends to represent our true interests—we must instead choose to believe God's Word. We must count on the realities about ourselves that God has pronounced. This attitude of faith will drastically affect what happens in our lives, for on this basis we'll be able to yield and obey in a new way.

Paul asks, "Since we have ended our relation to sin, how can we live in it any longer?" (Romans 6:2, Williams).

He reminds us that we died when Christ died, and our real life is hidden with Christ in God. Therefore we're to put to death the sinful, earthly things lurking within us (Colossians 3:3–5, NLT).

> "As far as this world is concerned, you are already dead, and your true life is a hidden one in God, through Christ."
>
> COLOSSIANS 3:3, PHILLIPS

No one who is born of God makes a practice of sinning, because the God-given life-principle continues to live in him, and so he cannot practice sinning, because he is born of God.

1 JOHN 3:9, WILLIAMS

Dead to Sin

❧

Thank You, Lord, for allowing me to become a partaker of Christ's death and all its benefits. Thank You that I've been acquitted from all my guilt, that I have "died to sin." I no longer live under sin's reign.

Thank You for the share I have in Christ's crucifixion and burial, just as I also share in His resurrection. It's a death and burial so real that it means I have actually been crucified with Your Son Jesus. I glory in the cross of Christ, because on that cross He satisfied the righteous demand of Your wrath against me because of my sins.

Reflect on what these passages say about your relationship to sin and death: Isaiah 25:7–8; Hosea 13:14; John 8:51; 1 Corinthians 15:26, 54–57; 2 Timothy 1:10; Hebrews 2:14–15; Revelation 20:14; 21:4

I want to continually rely on the facts that I'm both dead to sin and alive to You. Both facts, I know, are humanly impossible. But You, the God of the impossible, have made them realities, and I simply accept them by faith. I take You at Your word.

I acknowledge that any flirting with sin is absolutely inconsistent with who I really am—with my true identity in Christ. I acknowledge the truth that there's absolutely nothing about sin that is in any way helpful to my best interests, or even neutral. All sin is my enemy.

I ask for Your constant help in my lifelong responsibility of putting to death all that belongs to my sinful nature.

Thank You again that in Christ I'm dead to sin— but that it doesn't stop there. I'm also alive to You!

a LIBERATING separation

IN OUR FORMER identity, sin and death were the basic features of our nature. Sin was our alter ego, so much a part of us that we were one—inseparably one. We responded to sin and ignored the Lord; we were alive to sin and dead to God. We were guilty and condemned, enslaved in the very independence we so highly prized. We were slaves to sin and death, living under their relentless (though often velvet-gloved) rule. Sin was our nature and our master, and we yielded to it rather than to God.

Deep inside we viewed sin as our best friend and life partner, essential to a satisfying life. This was true of various specific sins, but especially of the basic sin of seeking independence from God. We wanted to be our own person in our own way, basing our confidence on our own merit and achievement.

> We ourselves were stupid and stubborn, dupes of sin, ordered every which way by our glands, going around with a chip on our shoulder, hated and hating back.
>
> TITUS 3:3, MESSAGE

What are some ways in your past in which you manifested the basic sin of seeking independence from God?

BUT NOW, through faith in Christ, we're to see ourselves in the light of the cross and the empty tomb. These are like a powerful blockade within us between who we were and who we have become—between our former realm of sin and guilt and death and our new realm of righteousness and life. The Cross is a gracious barrier between our new self and what remains of our old sinful desires and tendencies.

"Look upon yourselves as dead to the appeal and power of sin."
ROMANS 6:11, PHILLIPS

Being dead to sin doesn't mean that our "old self" no longer exists, but that it has been *separated* from our new and true self. In our innermost being we've been disconnected from sin, divorced from it. Sin is no longer our true nature, and we no longer need to submit to its mastery.

"Look upon your old sin nature as dead and unresponsive to sin."
ROMANS 6:11, TLB

Christ illustrates this for us. His role as the bearer of sin and death was ended by His death and resurrection, never again to be resumed. So in Him our own relationship to sin and death has been ended. In our true inner self sin is no longer our nature or our master.

"Consider yourselves as having ended your relation to sin."
ROMANS 6:11, WILLIAMS

Our death to sin was an event foreseen by God before the foundation of the world. It was also an event suffered by Christ at Calvary, and an event happening within us at the moment of our new birth. Being dead to sin and alive to God isn't fantasy, but fact. It is based on historical event. It's the way things really are in our genuine nature, in our innermost person, indwelt by the Holy Spirit, with Christ as our life. In Christ we have died to sin and we are alive to God.

IT'S NOT THAT sin no longer entices us. Sin fights against the Holy Spirit within us for control of our body and personality. And sin is cagey. It masquerades as a master who deserves our loyalty. It poses as our true nature, concerned about what's best for us. And if we yield to its demands or swallow its bait, it tries to either dull our conscience or plague us with guilt, whipping us even after we confess our sin to the Lord. In countless ways, sin seeks to cause distress, struggles, and defeats.

But from God's viewpoint, such sins are committed not by our true and new self, but by the doomed and disinherited sin that lingers within—"sin that dwells in me," as Paul described it from personal experience (Romans 7:17, 20, NKJV). Our sins spring from our old sinful tendencies that are no longer part of our true identity. The real you, the real me, hates sin and is aligned against it. The real us longs for our whole personality to be conformed to the image of Christ.

So the Scriptures emphasize the radical, night-and-day difference between the person we once were and the person we now are. As we cling to this truth, it can cut through the lingering attraction we may feel toward sin when temptations come. The real you is now and forever dead to sin and alive to God. Let's count on this!

The real you hates sin and is positioned against it. What convinces you that this is true? What need do you have to more fully confirm and embrace this truth?

A Liberating

We live according to the person we see ourselves to be. Romans 6 is *God's* exposé of what is true about us and what is true about sin in relation to us. This passage helps us see ourselves from God's viewpoint—as a new person who doesn't have to live under sin's rule, and who doesn't truly want to live there. God wants us to emphatically choose to believe this truth that He has revealed.

Father of all life, I gratefully acknowledge before You that I have ended my relationship with sin and guilt and death. And I have been born again, replacing that old relationship with an intimate, eternal relationship with You. How thrilling it is to know that because of my new birth I can relate to You in a totally new way.

When I walked in the flesh I was dominated by sin. But in Christ I'm free from that tyranny. I praise You that Your Life in me right now is infinitely greater and more powerful than sin.

Thank You again for ending my relationship to sin through the cross of Christ. I acknowledge before You that the real me hates sin and is aligned against it. The real me longs for my whole personality to be conformed to the image of Christ.

I praise You for Your holiness, Your hatred of sin. And I thank You for giving me new life, so that in the depths of my being I can—with You—share in that hatred. How grateful I am that, as I rely on You as my Life, I can do all that You want me to do!

Explore Romans 6 carefully. What does this rich passage confirm to you about the new person you now are in Christ?

Separation

UNITED WITH CHRIST

The words of Jesus: "You will know that I am in My Father, and you in Me, and I in you" (John 14:20, NKJV).

In the Father's presence, express to Him what it means to you that Christ is your life.

THE SUMMER I was eighteen, I spent much time soaking in Colossians 3. I sensed that something of tremendous importance was there and I got minor shafts of light. But I was still unable to grasp it.

That fall I experienced an inner dawning as I was reading a book that a Bible teacher recommended. I came across the following statement, based on Colossians 3:4: "It's not only true that my life is Christ's, but my life is Christ." Not only does my life belong to Christ, but also He *is* my life. He is living *His life* in and through me as I simply depend on Him. For Him to use me, I no longer need to depend on my ability. Instead I can depend on His working through me in such a way that at any given time He's using me (or not using me) as He sees best.

Time and again I still find release by simply praying, "Thank You, Lord, that Christ is my life!" And I pray for more and more depth and constancy in continuing to live by *His* life.

"CHRIST...is your real life," we read in Colossians 3:4 (NLT). This is true because God has infused you with the person and vitality of His Son. As you more and more come to understand who Christ is and what He's like—pure, holy, loving, powerful— you can praise Him that this is also what He is *in you.*

In this unity, you share in Christ's resurrection as well as in His crucifixion: "For if we have been united with Him in a death like His, then the same must be true of our resurrection with Him" (Romans 6:5, Berkeley). This sharing together means that you have been delivered out of Satan's "domain of darkness" (Colossians 1:13, ESV) and lifted into Christ's kingdom, where you're alive with the reality of your risen Lord. With Paul you can say, "My present life is not that of the old 'I,' but the living Christ within me" (Galatians 2:20, Phillips).

"Christ will be more and more at home in your hearts as you trust in him."

EPHESIANS 3:17, NLT

In a mystical but actual way, you are now one with God the Father as well as with Jesus His Son, just as Jesus promised: "If anyone loves me, he will keep my word, and my Father will love him, and we will come to him and make our home with him" (John 14:23, ESV).

We are in union with the True One through His Son, Jesus Christ. He is the true God and eternal life.

1 JOHN 5:20, WILLIAMS

BECAUSE YOU'RE alive with Christ's life, you're also righteous with His righteousness—for it's "in Christ" that you are "made good with the goodness of God" (2 Corinthians 5:21, Phillips).

It's not that God looks at you through Christ-colored glasses, but that He sees you as one with Christ in actual fact. You share His life and righteousness as your very own—as well as His glory (John 17:22). Your own life is "hidden with Christ in God" (Colossians 3:3).

Let your thoughts and emotions express these truths before God: Christ is my life, my wisdom, my righteousness, my sanctification, my redemption.

"God alone made it possible for you to be in Christ Jesus" (1 Corinthians 1:30, NLT), and in doing this for you He has also made Jesus to be your wisdom and righteousness and sanctification and redemption (1 Corinthians 1:30, ESV). Therefore you can say, "Christ is *my* wisdom, *my* righteousness, *my* sanctification, *my* redemption. I'm wise with His wisdom and righteous with His righteousness. By Him—by all that He is—I am sanctified and redeemed."

Christ and all that He is represents the only reason for the radical change in your identity. Therefore God gives you this thrilling invitation: "From now on you must grow stronger through union with the Lord and through His mighty power" (Ephesians 6:10, Williams). As you deepen and develop in this union, Jesus promises that your life will bear spiritual fruit: "It is the man who shares my life and whose life I share who proves fruitful" (John 15:5, Phillips).

United with Christ

⇛

*Lord Jesus, thank You that I have inner oneness
with You in the core of my being.*

*How grateful I am that You demonstrated in Your life on earth a
constant dependence on Your Father—and that I am to live and
serve with complete dependence on You as my indwelling Lord.
Open my eyes as I focus on Your life as You walked on earth.
May I in fresh ways behold Your glory, "the glory of the One and Only,
who came from the Father, full of grace and truth" (John 1:14, NIV).*

*What a delight to know that, as I fix my heart and eyes on You,
You continue by Your Holy Spirit to transform me into Your
image through my inner union with You.*

*And Father, I rejoice that, because of Your gift of life through Christ,
the impossible goal of being holy and acceptable to You has become a
reality in my life. How I rejoice that in the core of my being I've been
made righteous with Your righteousness and alive with your life.*

*Thank You again, Father, that both now and forever I'm united
with Your Son Jesus by Your indwelling Spirit. Blessed Trinity!*

1 Corinthians 1:30 shows that it is God's doing that we are in Christ. We're in God's favor because of what Christ has done, not because of our merits.

In view of this, Paul mentions a basic responsibility that the Lord assigns us: "Therefore, as it is written, 'Let the one who boasts, boast in the Lord'" (1 Corinthians 1:31, ESV).

Thanksgiving and praise are significant ways of "boasting in the Lord." Pause now for a time of praise and thanksgiving for the truths about God and about yourself that you've been focusing on in this book.

ONE WITH HIM
IN SPIRIT

IN OUR INNERMOST self, we're now one with Christ's Spirit, for "the person who is united to the Lord becomes one spirit with Him" (1 Corinthians 6:17, AMP). In our spirit we've been permanently fused with His own Spirit, and through this union all the other truths about who we are in Christ become realities.

In a vital way, in our true inner self, the qualities that are true of Christ are also true of us. We share His love, His holiness, and His submission to and reliance on His Father.

In contrast, before our new birth what is true of sin was true of us, because of our union with sin. Now we are linked with the Lord intimately and securely, and that's how He wants us to see ourselves.

This spiritual aspect of our union with Christ highlights the unique role of God's Holy Spirit in our new identity. After trusting Christ, we "were marked as belonging to Christ by the Holy Spirit, who long ago had been promised to all of us Christians" (Ephesians 1:13, TLB). So our body is now the temple of the Holy Spirit who is in us, whom we have from God (1 Corinthians 6:19).

"With his Spirit living in you, your body will be as alive as Christ's!"

ROMANS 8:11, MESSAGE

"The Spirit of him who raised Christ Jesus from the dead…will, by that same Spirit, bring to your whole being new strength and vitality."

ROMANS 8:11, PHILLIPS

As BELIEVERS we are spiritually one with Christ, and He is one with God the Father and the Holy Spirit. So the Bible speaks of all three members of the Trinity living within every believer.

Regarding God the Father, the apostle John wrote, "If anyone acknowledges that Jesus is the Son of God, God lives in him and he in God. And so we know and rely on the love God has for us" (1 John 4:15–16, NIV).

Regarding the Holy Spirit, we're assured that "God has sent forth the Spirit of His Son into our hearts, crying, 'Abba! Father!'" (Galatians 4:6, NASB).

The Scriptures also teach us that Christ the Son lives in us. "This is the secret: Christ lives in you, and this is your assurance that you will share in his glory" (Colossians 1:27, NLT). "Christ lives in me," Paul proclaimed with confidence (Galatians 2:20)—and so can we.

Just think: We are indwelt by the fullness of God Himself—the triune God! As we simply choose to trust Him, He is revealed in us, magnified in our bodies.

> The Spirit of God, who raised Jesus from the dead, lives in you. And just as he raised Christ from the dead, he will give life to your mortal body by this same Spirit living within you.
>
> ROMANS 8:11, NLT

"The people who live on the plane of the lower nature cannot please God. But you are not living on the plane of the lower nature, but on the spiritual plane, if the Spirit of God has His home within you. Unless a man has the Spirit of Christ, he does not belong to Him."

ROMANS 8:8–9, WILLIAMS

Take God at His word. Accept it as true that you are indwelt with the fullness of God Himself, that His Spirit has His home within you and you belong to Him. In a special time of fellowship with the Lord, express to Him what this means to you.

OUR ONENESS with Christ through the Spirit is rooted in the Lord's faithfulness to His promises. Centuries before Christ's birth, God promised His people, "I will put my Spirit within you, and cause you to walk in my statutes and be careful to obey my rules" (Ezekiel 36:27, ESV).

Now with the Spirit having been poured out upon us, "His presence within us is God's guarantee that he really will give us all that he promised; and the Spirit's seal upon us means that God has already purchased us and that he guarantees to bring us to himself. This is just one more reason for us to praise our glorious God" (Ephesians 1:14, TLB).

The reality of the Spirit also confirms Christ's own promises. With the Spirit in mind, He said, "Whoever continues to believe in Me will have, as the Scripture says, rivers of living water continuously flowing from within" (John 7:38, Williams). And concerning "the Spirit of truth," Jesus made this promise to His disciples: "He is going to remain with you, and will be within you" (John 14:17, Williams).

> You are the temple of the living God. As God has said: "I will dwell in them and walk among them. I will be their God, and they shall be My people."
>
> 2 CORINTHIANS 6:16, NKJV

What truths about the Holy Spirit most inspire you to praise the Lord?

Take time to genuinely thank the Lord that He has been faithful to His promises to give you the Holy Spirit and a vital new life.

One with Him

*What a joy it is, Lord, to know that my spirit
has been permanently fused with Your Spirit!*

*Thank You for the sealing of Your Holy Spirit that marks me as Yours
forever! Thank You for the incredible privilege of allowing my body,
here and now, to actually be a temple of Your Holy Spirit.
Rivers of living water can now flow freely and continuously
from within me, all because Your Spirit indwells my spirit.
What good news this is!*

*I praise You for being faithful to Your ancient promises regarding Your
Spirit. How incredibly loving You are to actually fill us with Yourself!*

Thank You again, in Jesus' name, that I am one with You in Spirit.

"This is what the LORD says…: It is not by force nor by strength, but by my Spirit, says the LORD Almighty."
ZECHARIAH 4:6, NLT

"Let the Holy Spirit fill and control you."
EPHESIANS 5:18, NLT

Reflect on the truths in the following passages about experiencing the fullness of the Holy Spirit:
Joel 2:28–29;
Luke 11:13; Acts 2:1–4;
2:16–21; 6:3, 5; 11:24;
Galatians 5:22–23;
2 Timothy 1:7

in Spirit

fiLLeD

The words of Jesus:
"My purpose is to give
life in all its fullness"
(John 10:10, NLT).

Express to the Lord
your gratitude for the
fullness which you
know—by faith—is
yours. Talk with Him as
well about your
longings to experience
this with greater
constancy and intensity.

As believers in Christ, we have actually been united with Him through the Spirit of God. What an immense privilege! How can it mean anything less for us than rich inner fulfillment and fullness?

Such fullness is indeed ours, and God wants us to experience it with grateful and growing awareness. He moved Paul to write, "Praise be to…God…for giving us through Christ every possible spiritual benefit as citizens of Heaven!" (Ephesians 1:3, Phillips). Paul also says we've been given the Holy Spirit "that we might realize and comprehend and appreciate the gifts of divine favor and blessing so freely and lavishly bestowed on us by God" (1 Corinthians 2:12, AMP).

"As we know Jesus better, his divine power gives us everything we need for living a godly life" (2 Peter 1:3, NLT). In Christ each of us literally has all that is necessary for fullness of life, for attaining and enjoying God's high purposes for us.

What more can we need than the fullness of Christ? "For all things are yours…and you are Christ's, and Christ is God's" (1 Corinthians 3:21, 23, ESV).

THIS FULLNESS drives out any sense of being empty or incomplete or lacking purpose. So we're able to affirm with David, "My cup overflows" (Psalm 23:5).

This overflow manifests itself in joy, as we acknowledge with David, "In your presence there is fullness of joy" (Psalm 16:11, ESV). And we can say with Paul, "This doesn't mean, of course, that we have only a hope of future joys—we can be full of joy here and now even in our trials and troubles" (Romans 5:3, Phillips). We can hold on to the promise of Jesus: "You will be filled with my joy. Yes, your joy will overflow!" (John 15:11, NLT).

Our fullness is a practical one, extending to every aspect of daily life: "God is able to provide you with every blessing in abundance, so that you may always have enough of everything and may provide in abundance for every good work" (2 Corinthians 9:8, RSV).

Our enrichment points us to Christ's own fullness—for "He was full of unfailing love and faithfulness" (John 1:14, NLT). "And from his fullness we have all received, grace upon grace" (John 1:16, ESV). In Christ "the whole fullness of deity dwells bodily, and you have been filled in him, who is the head of all rule and authority" (Colossians 2:9–10, ESV).

> "May the God of hope fill you with joy and peace in your faith, that by the power of the Holy Spirit, your whole life and outlook may be radiant with hope."
>
> ROMANS 15:13, PHILLIPS

PAUL'S PRAYERS often point the way to the fullness we can experience. We can be "filled with all the fullness of God," "filled with the fruit of righteousness that comes through Jesus Christ, to the glory and praise of God," and "filled with the knowledge of his will in all spiritual wisdom and understanding" (Ephesians 3:19, NKJV; Philippians 1:11, ESV; Colossians 1:9, ESV).

In Christ we have a rich and full supply of grace, peace, forgiveness, wisdom, nourishment, strength, light, comfort—all that we need for abundant living, whatever our circumstances may be.

God has endowed us with this abundance not for independent use or for self-exalting ends, for we are not our own. We're to use for good our overflowing gifts, letting God use them to make us more like His Son—more holy, more beautiful, more honoring to our Father. They are ours to prepare us for our incredible destiny of sharing God's glory—of becoming "everlasting splendors," perfect in beauty and shining like the stars forever (C. S. Lewis, *The Weight of Glory*).

The Lord dwells in us and we in Him—and He desires to dwell there ever more fully. Our continuing aim is to be "mature and full grown in the Lord, measuring up to the full stature of Christ" (Ephesians 4:13, NLT).

The fullness, the many blessings that you've been given—how does God want you to use them in service to Him and service to others?

Filled

Father, although in the flesh I'm proud and self-serving,
I accept my position in Christ as a created being,
in total need of You, glorying in You alone.

In myself I'm empty and incomplete, but in Your Son
I'm filled and complete. I'm lacking nothing, because He
more than compensates for my lack at every point of need.

Because of the love You have lavished upon me, my life overflows
with Your blessings. You fill and satisfy me. You grant
me everything I need. You enflame my heart with joy.

More and more may my fullness from You overflow in love and praise
to You and in love and service to those around me—my brothers
and sisters in Christ and those who do not yet know You.

Thank You again that in Christ I am filled to overflowing.

For your further reflection on the fullness that is yours in Christ, turn to Psalms 36:7–9; 63:5–6; Isaiah 25:6; 55:1; Jeremiah 31:12–14; John 4:14; I Timothy 1:13–14.

always a receiver

26

THE POSITIVE truths about our fullness in Christ are humbling, for all of them are ours by God's amazing grace, which we in no way deserve.

It's not because of our own merits that we're vibrantly alive, richly endowed, and assured of a destiny far beyond imagining. It's only because of Christ's merits.

> "Every good gift and every perfect gift is from above, and comes down from the Father of lights."
>
> JAMES 1:17, NKJV

God is the Giver, the Source of the abundant grace that brings us every spiritual blessing in Christ. So each of us is basically a receiver, not an independent achiever. And this is true not only in salvation but also in every aspect of our lives.

As we feed on God's Word, the Holy Spirit enlightens us to grasp these truths and their significance. This enables us to hold our heads high not in pride but in humble gratitude, submission, and dependence. As our awareness of God's grace deepens, we can repeatedly confess with Jacob, "I am not worthy of all the faithfulness and unfailing love you have shown to me" (Genesis 32:10, NLT).

IN CHRIST we stand permanently in God's unmerited favor. We are receivers of a full and steady overflow that is not limited by our failures, for where sin abounds, grace abounds much more (Romans 5:20, NKJV).

Yet God's grace in no way encourages us to sin. As we view grace in the light of God's gracious, life-transforming purposes, it frees us from false beliefs that keep us in sin's grip. Grace cuts through an especially thick layer in our old identity—namely seeing ourselves as persons who must earn God's favor (as if we could!). The truth about grace cuts through our pride of achievement. Yet it gives us a positive basis for a strong sense of identity, for it lets us know that we are highly favored in God's eyes, now and forever. Viewing ourselves under grace both humbles and uplifts us.

So we're to keep clearly in mind that we are under grace. We're not to forget that grace is our new environment, the new place in which we live, and our new basis for being approved. We're approved on the basis of what Christ has done and who He has made us through our new birth. We're not to let sin sneak in the back door by seeing ourselves as needing to win approval through self-effort—through what we do in our own power.

We can boldly affirm with Paul, "Whatever I am now, it is all because God poured out his special favor on me." And this is not without results—results that happen because God works through us by his grace (1 Corinthians 15:10, NLT).

THE HOLY SPIRIT wants to saturate our minds with the truths of His fullness and grace that He has revealed in the Bible. As we meditate on these truths and respond with praise, He delivers us from feeling we must beg God for what He has already given us. He wants us to pray with understanding and with praise.

Are there ways you have been pleading for gifts from God which He has, in fact, already promised and provided? If you can recall such prayers, pause now to change them to expressions of gratefulness to Him.

There's no need, for example, to beg for victory when Christ within us is already our more-than-conquering life.

There's no need to plead for the Holy Spirit's presence as though He were not already indwelling us and yearning for us to let Him fill and control us and produce His fruit in our lives.

There's no need to cry to the Lord for spiritual and emotional resources as though these can be ours only as extra bonuses. We forget that they are part of our birthright in Christ.

In Colossians 2:6, Paul tells us that we're to live in Christ in the same way in which we first received Him as our Lord and Savior. We first received Him by being humble enough to face and admit our need for Him, and then by simply believing in Him, as John 1:12 makes clear. Then the continuing reality of living in Christ likewise means active faith in Him—choosing to believe that His grace and power can meet our every need in all of our living and serving. And we activate our faith by praising Him.

Always a Receiver

*I praise You, Lord, for how gracious You are—generous
beyond imagining! You don't give reluctantly, for You delight
to do good to each of Your beloved children.*

*The abundance of Your grace—Your unmerited favor—
makes my heart sing for joy. You offered me eternal life,
now and forever, and I have gladly received it. You offered me oneness
with Your Son through the Holy Spirit, and I have gladly received it.*

*When I sin You offer me forgiveness,
and I gladly receive Your inner cleansing.*

*In Christ You offer me love and wisdom and strength,
and I gladly receive them. Day by day You offer me all that I
need for life and godliness. May I gratefully open myself to
receive with thanksgiving all that You provide.*

*I give thanks to You, for You are good,
and Your steadfast love endures forever (Psalm 136:1).*

Look up the following passages to explore God's generosity and the rich gifts He prepares for you to receive, practical as well as spiritual. Psalms 81:10, 16; 145:7–9, 15–16; Proverbs 2:6; Zechariah 10:1; Matthew 5:44–45; 7:8; John 1:9; Acts 14:16–17

new altogether

ALLOW YOUR thinking to be absorbed with this truth: In Christ you have become "a new person altogether—the past is finished and gone, everything has become fresh and new" (2 Corinthians 5:17, Phillips). You've been given a new life, a new heredity, a new nature. In your innermost being you're a new person.

> "What counts is whether we really have been changed into new and different people."
>
> GALATIANS 6:15, NLT

Along with believers in Christ everywhere, you can enjoy all the qualities of this new life in Christ, for "He saved us through the washing of rebirth and renewal by the Holy Spirit" (Titus 3:5, NIV).

So take God at His word and press forward into a growing experience of the renewal to which He has called you.

> What kinds of "oldness" might still be lingering in your thought patterns and attitudes? To replace them, God's truth about your newness is yours to fully embrace. Ask Him to help you do this.

In *The Pursuit of God,* A. W. Tozer wrote that when we decide firmly to honor the Lord with our lives, "we step out of the world's parade.... We acquire a new viewpoint; a new and different psychology will be formed within us; a new power will begin to surprise us by its upsurgings and its outgoings." All this newness is yours!

"I will give you a new heart with new and right desires."

EZEKIEL 36:26, NLT

THE MOMENT you die, your spirit and your personality—the new and true you—will immediately go to be "at home with the Lord" (2 Corinthians 5:8, NIV). You'll leave behind all your sinful tendencies, all your old patterns of living. And when Christ returns, He'll give you a new body, totally free from even the slightest remnant of sin and death. Your new body will be "imperishable" and "supernatural," it will be "raised in honor and glory," and it will be "resurrected in strength and endued with power" (1 Corinthians 15:42–44, AMP).

Think of the freedom from sin's guilt and power which you will then experience! Imagine the total way you'll be dead to sin and alive to God!

Then let this truth dawn on you: In your innermost being, as a "new creation" through Christ's life in you, this has already happened to you spiritually! It isn't make-believe. God says it is true, and so it is.

> You have stripped off your old evil nature and all its wicked deeds. In its place you have clothed yourselves with a brand-new nature that is continually being renewed as you learn more and more about Christ, who created this new nature within you.
>
> COLOSSIANS 3:9–10, NLT

> The old condition has passed away, a new condition has come.
>
> 2 CORINTHIANS 5:17, WILLIAMS

"Behold, I will do something new, now it will spring forth; will you not be aware of it?"

ISAIAH 43:19, NASB

As you look at one or more of the truths mentioned in these pages about who you are in Christ, you may sometimes think to yourself, "Well, that's just not true of me, even though I belong to Christ." In reaching that conclusion, which part of you are you identifying with? With the dynamics and patterns that ruled you before you knew Christ, the old bankrupt qualities that remain within you? Or with the true, new you?

GOD WANTS us to count on the fact that we have a new nature and identity, and that we can continually grow in our experience of all that this newness means.

Actively thanking and praising God for these facts will help you see yourself as God sees you. As you do this, these truths do not merely make you feel better. They also lay the groundwork for a life of fuller obedience.

Praise the Lord often for the massive difference He has made in you through your new birth and the new, eternal, spiritual life that is yours in Christ. Such praise can help you view yourself honestly and therefore live the new life God has in mind for you.

The basis for this is always found in Jesus. Visualize Him risen through the glory of the Father, forever beyond the condemning power of our sin which crucified Him. His life is "an indestructible life" (Hebrews 7:16, NIV). He tells us, "I am the Living One; I was dead, and behold I am alive for ever and ever!" (Revelation 1:18, NIV).

And what is true of Him is true of each of us in our spirit. His resurrected life is ours to live out today and forever. We have risen indeed!

"And He who sits on the throne said, 'Behold, I am making all things new.... These words are faithful and true.'"

REVELATION 21:5, NASB

Just as Christ rose from the dead through the Father's glorious power, so we too shall conduct ourselves in a new way of living.

ROMANS 6:4, BERKELEY

New Altogether

How I praise You, my loving Father, that I've been born into Your family by receiving Your only begotten Son—by believing in Him as my Savior. I've been born out of the old and into the new!

I thank You for Your promise to provide both the desire and the power to live a new life. Thank You, Father, for who I now am in spirit …and for what I shall be in totality in my eternal future.

I rejoice that I am a new person, resurrected in spirit! Thank You for grafting Your nature and Your Son's resurrected life into my spirit, so that now I can increasingly experience resurrection reality in my daily life. I no longer need to let sin reign in me. I need not yield to sin because I can yield to You. I can choose against the old and for the new, as a spiritually dead person raised to newness of life. How grateful I am for this new freedom!

So I thank You again, Father, that in Christ I'm a new person. "The old has gone, the new has come!" (2 Corinthians 5:17, NIV).

Think about the newness you're called to by meditating on these passages. Romans 6:19, 22; 7:6; 12:1–2; 13:13–14; 2 Corinthians 4:16; Ephesians 4:22–24; Colossians 2:11–12; 1 John 2:6

empowered

Our inner union with our all-powerful Christ energizes us for a life of obedience and service. We're not to think of ourself as fettered, defeated, or inadequate, but as someone who is backed by power and authority, someone who is impregnated with the all-powerful life of Christ.

Paul tells us, "The Christ you have to deal with is not a weak person outside you, but a tremendous power inside you. He was 'weak' enough to be crucified, yes, but he lives now by the power of God" (2 Corinthians 13:3–4, Phillips).

Where do you most need the Lord's energy in your life at this time?

We have inside us "the same mighty power that raised Christ from the dead and seated him in the place of honor at God's right hand in the heavenly realms" (Ephesians 1:19–20, NLT).

In Christ, God Himself "is at work within you, giving you the will and the power to achieve his purpose" (Philippians 2:13, Phillips). Therefore we can say, "The LORD God is my strength; He will make my feet like deer's feet, and He will make me walk on my high hills" (Habakkuk 3:19, NKJV).

IN CHRIST we can count on having all the energy we truly need. "I have strength for all things in Christ Who empowers me—I am ready for anything and equal to anything through Him Who infuses inner strength into me; I am self-sufficient in Christ's sufficiency" (Philippians 4:13, AMP).

Here again Paul's prayers point the way. Out of God's "glorious, unlimited resources" we can receive "mighty inner strength through his Holy Spirit" (Ephesians 3:16, NLT). He makes it possible for us to be "strengthened with all power, according to His glorious might, for the attaining of all steadfastness and patience" (Colossians 1:11, NASB).

Paul also reminds us that, "according to the power that works in us," the Almighty God "is able to do exceedingly abundantly above all that we ask or think" (Ephesians 3:20, NKJV). His active power can do infinitely more than you or I can ever hope for or dream of.

> "Those who were weak are now strong."
>
> 1 SAMUEL 2:4, NLT

So He comes to us as He came to Daniel, saying, "Peace be to you; be strong, yes, be strong!" (Daniel 10:19, NKJV).

He comes to us as He came to Paul, saying, "My grace is sufficient for you, for My strength is made perfect in weakness"; and we can respond with Paul, "When I am weak, then I am strong" (2 Corinthians 12:9–10, NKJV).

He gives power to the weak, and to those who have no might He increases strength.

ISAIAH 40:29, NKJV

AS WE LABOR in the tasks God assigns us, and as we face the suffering He allows, we can look to Him and His grace for enabling. We can say as Paul did, "I exert all my strength in reliance upon the power of Him who is mightily at work within me" (Colossians 1:29, Weymouth).

Therefore we're to actively seek—and find—our strength in the Lord. We're to hear His invitation: "Search for the LORD and for his strength, and keep on searching" (1 Chronicles 16:11, NLT). "Trust in the LORD forever, for in YAH, the LORD, is everlasting strength" (Isaiah 26:4, NKJV).

Hearing such an invitation, we can respond to the Lord with grateful praise, "You have been a stronghold to the poor, a stronghold to the needy in his distress" (Isaiah 25:4, ESV). "My flesh and my heart may fail, but God is the strength of my heart and my portion forever" (Psalm 73:26, NIV).

The reality of the Lord's strength means that in Him we find for ourselves a solid support, even in the most difficult circumstances.

"In quietness and confidence shall be your strength."

ISAIAH 30:15, NKJV

"The joy of the LORD is your strength."

NEHEMIAH 8:10

> "This precious treasure—this light and power that now shine within us—is held in perishable containers, that is, in our weak bodies. So everyone can see that our glorious power is from God and is not our own."
>
> 2 CORINTHIANS 4:7, NLT

> "The LORD is the source of all my righteousness and strength."
>
> ISAIAH 45:24, NLT

> "Be strong in the grace that is in Christ Jesus."
>
> 2 TIMOTHY 2:1

Empowered

How I rejoice, Lord, that "In your hand are power and might,
and in your hand it is to make great and to give strength to all"
(1 Chronicles 29:12, ESV).

Almighty God, thank You that through my union with Christ I've
been resurrected into a new life and identity. Through Him I can
experience power and enabling beyond what I have ever known.

Thank You that I no longer need to be anxious, for in Christ
I am adequate…enabled…empowered. Anxiety and fear are
no longer realistic, for in You I have every reason
to be confident, trusting, and at rest.

So my heart rejoices in You, the strongest Strong One,
as my constant source of energy and strength and protection.

"I have strength for all things in Christ Who empowers me—I am
ready for anything and equal to anything through Him Who infuses
inner strength into me; I am self-sufficient in Christ's sufficiency"
(Philippians 4:13, AMP).

Look to the Lord and
His strength by turning
to these additional
Scriptures:
Exodus 15:6;
Psalm 18:1; 46:1; 103:5;
Isaiah 12:2; 40:30–31;
Zechariah 10:12;
Matthew 14:27

eNLIGHTeNeD

THROUGH CHRIST'S indwelling presence we go from being "full of darkness" to being "full of light" (Luke 11:34–36). For example, this is true of our self-image—of our sense of who we are and who we will be forever. Christ delivers us from the darkness of our distorted ideas about ourselves into a clear and shining understanding of reality.

"God, who first ordered light to shine in darkness, has flooded our hearts with his light" (2 Corinthians 4:6, Phillips). In Christ our eyes were opened so we could turn "from darkness to light and from the power of Satan to God" (Acts 26:18, ESV).

This enlightenment means that we are special people, for "God's secret plan has now been revealed to us…a plan centered on Christ" (Ephesians 1:9, NLT). For "God's mystery…is Christ, in whom are hidden all the treasures of wisdom and knowledge" (Colossians 2:2–3, ESV). "His Spirit searches out everything and shows us even God's deep secrets" (1 Corinthians 2:10, NLT).

Therefore Jesus tells us, "To you it has been given to know the secrets of the kingdom of heaven" (Matthew 13:11, ESV). "Blessed are your eyes," He says, "because they see" (Matthew 13:16, NIV). What privileged people we are!

"Light dawns in the darkness for the upright."

PSALM 112:4, ESV

PAUL REFERS to "the eyes of your heart" being "enlightened" (Ephesians 1:18, NASB). This means a bright new understanding of our life and purpose, for "the path of the righteous is like the light of dawn, which shines brighter and brighter until full day" (Proverbs 4:18, ESV).

Listen to the Lord's bright promises:

"I will lead the blind in a way that they do not know, in paths that they have not known I will guide them. I will turn the darkness before them into light" (Isaiah 42:16, ESV).

"The LORD will be to you an everlasting light" (Isaiah 60:19, NKJV).

"Out of their gloom and darkness the eyes of the blind shall see" (Isaiah 29:18, ESV).

"The people walking in darkness have seen a great light; on those living in the land of the shadow of death a light has dawned" (Isaiah 9:2, NIV).

So we learn to richly praise the Lord as David does: "The LORD is my light and my salvation" (Psalm 27:1).

And we can say, "Though I fall, I will rise again. Though I sit in darkness, the LORD himself will be my light" (Micah 7:8, NLT).

"Your word is a lamp to my feet and a light to my path."

PSALM 119:105, ESV

"The unfolding of your words gives light."

PSALM 119:130, ESV

What light for your current circumstances and responsibilities is God faithfully giving you at this time?

God is Light, and in Him there is no darkness at all.

1 JOHN 1:5, NASB

In Your light we see light.

PSALM 36:9, NKJV

JESUS TELLS US, "You are the light of the world" (Matthew 5:14). This is possible only because of who Jesus is within us— for He says, "I am the light of the world" (John 8:12, ESV). He explains, "I have come as Light into the world, so that everyone who believes in Me will not remain in darkness" (John 12:46, NASB). He promises, "Believe in the light…then you will become children of the light" (John 12:36, NLT). And God "has made us understand that this light is the brightness of the glory of God that is seen in the face of Jesus Christ" (2 Corinthians 4:6, NLT).

His light can now radiate from us. "It is for you now to demonstrate the goodness of him who has called you out of darkness into his amazing light" (1 Peter 2:9, Phillips). "For at one time you were darkness itself, but now in union with the Lord you are light itself. You must live like children of light, for the product of light consists in practicing everything that is good, and right, and true" (Ephesians 5:8–9, Williams).

A shining clarity is now possible in our thoughts and in our actions: "Let us who live in the light think clearly" (1 Thessalonians 5:8, NLT). "Walk in the Light as He Himself is in the Light" (1 John 1:7, NASB).

> "For you are all children of the light and of the day; we don't belong to darkness and night."
>
> I THESSALONIANS 5:5, NLT

Enlightened

⤜⤛

You are light, Lord, the One in whom there is no darkness at all
(1 John 1:5). I glorify You, for as I follow You I shall not walk
in darkness, because I have the light of life—everlasting light
(John 8:12; Isaiah 60:19).

Thank You for how Your light shines through Your Son, who is Himself
the bright radiance, the flawless expression of Your glory (Hebrews 1:3).
He is the light that has conquered my darkness.
He is the light that overcomes my fears (Psalm 27:1).

I praise You, Father, that Your spiritual light is like sunshine
in my life, warming my inner being and allowing my mind
and heart to see what You want me to see. Thank You for
the light of Your guidance, shining on my pathway.

I praise You that in You I am enlightened. How grateful I am
that You have called me out of darkness into Your marvelous light,
that I may show forth Your excellencies (1 Peter 2:9).

Study carefully
I Thessalonians 5:4–11
to grasp more firmly
what your transition
from darkness to light
really means.

three pillars
of your
new identity

Part Three

BeLONGING

Think about your need to feel that you belong, that you are worthy, and that you are competent. How fundamental do these qualities seem to be in your sense of identity?

Learn to take a clear mental snapshot of your positive experiences and any feelings of belongingness, worthiness, and competence they give you. Think about them and let your good feelings rise with gratefulness to God. Store them in your inner album where they can repeatedly give you emotional support.

Memorizing key verses is a great way to store them for frequent use.

In *THE SENSATION of Being Somebody,* pioneer Christian counselor Dr. Maurice Wagner identified a triad of feelings—belongingness, worthiness, and competence. These work together like the legs of a tripod to support our self-concept.

Of these three feelings, Wagner wrote that belongingness is primary and fundamental to developing the other two. *Belongingness* is the sense of being accepted and included by people important to us—feeling needed and desired by them.

Worthiness, meanwhile, is feeling that we are good and right, that we're clean and forgiven and honorable.

And *competence* is an "I can" feeling about what we want or need to accomplish in our lives.

I find that these three "pillars" are helpful in looking further at our self-identity. They help us see how wonderfully Christ can meet our identity needs. They also help us discern how we typically, apart from Christ, try to satisfy our emotional needs through our own efforts and through the mirror of how other people view us.

BELONGINGNESS IS a sense of being wanted and enjoyed, of being cared for and needed. It's a feeling of togetherness—a "we" feeling.

Psychologists have emphasized our basic human need to find a place for ourselves through relationships—through belongingness. Few of us would argue with the finding that for psychological wholeness, we must have at least one person who cares about us and whom we ourselves care for.

The opposite of belongingness is feeling alienated, rejected, excluded, or ignored. When we harbor any form of hostility in our hearts—such as anger, resentment, envy, hatred, mental argument—we block our sense of belongingness even with people who truly love us.

How would you assess the deep importance of your own need for belongingness?

On the human level we base our feelings of belongingness on our ability to attract love and approval and inclusion. Since both we and other people are imperfect and changeable, human relationships fail to fully meet our need for inner support.

In God we have a belongingness based on eternal, unconditional love—love that accepts us without regard for our merits or demerits. He has welcomed us into a union with Himself that transcends all others in intimacy and permanence. Along with every believer of all ages, we are children of the Father, the bride of the Son, and the temple in which the Holy Spirit dwells.

IN THE BOOK of Colossians, Paul spoke against a heresy in which some claimed a special enlightenment through secret knowledge. This led them to view others as deficient outsiders.

But in Christ we never have to view ourselves as deficient or as outsiders, or as inferior to those who see themselves as exclusive or elite. We already belong in the special group that matters most. We qualify simply because Christ is in us (Colossians 1:27).

At what times or in what circumstances are you most tempted to view yourself as an outsider, or as deficient compared to others?

Now we belong to Christ Jesus (Ephesians 2:13, NLT). We are Christ's, and Christ is God's (1 Corinthians 3:23, ESV). Through Christ we belong to the God of all the universe, the ultimate source of belongingness.

"Through the blood of Christ" we are now "inside the circle of God's love" (Ephesians 2:13, Phillips). We "belong in God's household with every other Christian" (Ephesians 2:19, TLB). Each of us is a full member of "the church of the firstborn, whose names are written in heaven" (Hebrews 12:23, NIV).

Such belongingness from God begins to give purpose to life, wrote Maurice Wagner. "All at once you're hooked up to His purpose, past and present. You're hooked up to eternity. You sense His hand on you, His loving caress around your heart. You feel plugged in to life because you've found your identity in God. God plus man makes the complete person, not man alone."

Belonging

*Loving Father, thank You for supplying everything I need in
my sense of who I am. You supply it as I let You relate to me,
and as I learn to know You better.*

*Thank You for wanting me and for bringing me to Yourself for Your
own enjoyment and glory. I'm Yours! I belong to the Almighty God
of the universe! What a thrill this is—and what a soothing remedy
for the times when I'm tempted to feel alienated or excluded or
ignored by others. I always have You, and I'll always belong to You.*

*I praise You for Your rich love that has welcomed me into a
union with Yourself, a union which transcends all others
in intimacy and permanence. In Your eyes I will never be
an outsider, but always an insider.*

*Thank You for bringing me inside the circle of Your love and purpose.
Thank You for Your Church which is my eternal family and
household and nation. I rejoice in the warm embrace of
belongingness that surrounds me—all because of You!*

What does belonging to the Lord—being truly and fully His—mean to you? Reflect on that question by exploring these passages: Psalms 79:13; 95:6–7; Isaiah 40:11; Ezekiel 34:11, 30–31; John 10:14–16, 27–30; 1 Peter 2:9

accepted

As someone who is in Christ, you belong to God as His very own. You are fully accepted by Him. "He made us accepted in the Beloved" (Ephesians 1:6, NKJV). "He has accepted you because of what the Lord Jesus Christ and the Spirit of our God have done for you" (1 Corinthians 6:11, TLB).

God doesn't accept people because they "measure up"—because they are innocent or strong or admirable. As Jesus taught, God gladly associates with anyone who is willing to admit his sin and his spiritual need. And He establishes a permanent relationship with those who honestly seek His deliverance, a relationship that excludes the possibility of being rejected. As Jesus said, "Those the Father has given me will come to me, and I will never reject them" (John 6:37, NLT).

In Christ you are both accepted and approved. Your righteousness in Him is a position of approval and this approval brings peace. "Having been justified by faith, we have peace with God through our Lord Jesus Christ" (Romans 5:1, NKJV).

"Because of Christ and our faith in him, we can now come fearlessly into God's presence, assured of his glad welcome."

EPHESIANS 3:12, NLT

"Can we boast, then, that we have done anything to be accepted by God? No."

ROMANS 3:27, NLT

HOW AMAZING it is that God fully accepts us even though He also fully knows us—our weaknesses, sinfulness, and all. He is intimately acquainted with all our ways (Psalm 139:3, NASB). "For He knows our frame; He remembers that we are dust" (Psalm 103:14, NKJV). Yet He accepts us now and forever.

God's full acceptance and knowledge of us means that we can fully trust Him: "For how well he understands us and knows what is best for us at all times" (Ephesians 1:8, TLB). What a loving Father we have!

God continually accepts us because we are righteous in Christ. This means we can come into His presence and be heard at any time. "When the righteous cry for help, the LORD hears and delivers them out of all their troubles" (Psalm 34:17, ESV). "If we ask anything according to his will he hears us" (1 John 5:14, ESV). "He hears the prayer of the righteous" (Proverbs 15:29, NASB).

So He warmly invites us to come and keep on coming: "Pour out your heart before Him; God is a refuge for us" (Psalm 62:8, NASB). "Come boldly to the throne of our gracious God. There we will receive his mercy, and we will find grace to help us when we need it" (Hebrews 4:16, NLT).

> "Accept one another, then, just as Christ accepted you, in order to bring praise to God."
>
> ROMANS 15:7, NIV

As you reflect on the full acceptance which both you and other believers have from God, how does this help you love them more?

Does it break down barriers in your heart?

OUR BELONGINGNESS in Christ brings us many new pictures of ourselves that become powerful elements of our new identity— bold new captions that God gives for our inner identity album. In the Bible, He takes the beautiful relationships of human life (such as father, bridegroom, husband, friend) and says, "I am *that* to you, and more; I'm that to you in its ideal form."

> "How great is the love the Father has lavished on us, that we should be called children of God! And that is what we are!"
>
> 1 JOHN 3:1, NIV

Belonging to God means you can embrace with certainty the truth that you really are His son or daughter. Jesus is "the firstborn, with many brothers and sisters" (Romans 8:29, NLT)—and you're one of them, as someone "born of the Spirit" (John 3:6). For "to all who received him, to those who believed in his name, he gave the right to become the children of God" (John 1:12, NIV).

God assures us, "I will be a Father to you, and you shall be My sons and daughters, says the LORD Almighty" (2 Corinthians 6:18, NKJV). And through His Spirit, He keeps intensifying our personal experience of His fatherhood: "And because you are sons, God has sent the Spirit of His Son into your hearts, crying, 'Abba,' that is, 'Father.' So you are no longer a slave, but a son; and if a son, then an heir by God's own act" (Galatians 4:6–7, Williams).

> How does the Holy Spirit intensify your personal experience of being a child of God?

For all who are led by the Spirit of God are sons of God.

ROMANS 8:14, ESV

Accepted

Lord of heaven and earth, how I praise You that You are my perfect Father who fully accepts me as Your child through Christ, Your only begotten Son.

Thank You that through Your Son I have Your approval. By His sacrifice I can enter Your presence at any time, day or night, assured that You welcome and gladly hear me. So I come before You now to thank and praise and worship You.

I rejoice in the refuge I find in You, Father—a safe refuge where I receive mercy for my failures and grace to help in every time of need. You are better to me than all I could ever hope for or dream of.

By Your Spirit within me, my heart cries out and calls You "Abba"— my dear and loving Father.

Soak your heart and mind in the truths of being God's child by reflecting on these passages: Matthew 5:44–45, 48; John 1:12–13; Romans 8:15–17; 2 Corinthians 6:17–18; Hebrews 2:10; 4:16

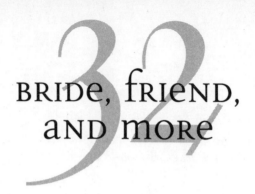

bride, friend, and more

"How sweet is your love, my sister, my bride; how much more delicious is your love than wine; and the fragrance of your ointments than all the rich spices."

SONG OF SOLOMON 4:10,
BERKELEY

THE WONDERFUL and many-sided belongingness which God provides means that each of us can actually think of ourself as His bride, as Scripture encourages us to do. "For your Maker is your husband, the LORD of hosts is his name" (Isaiah 54:5, ESV).

The Lord has promised His people: "I will betroth you to Me forever; yes, I will betroth you to Me in righteousness and justice, in lovingkindness and mercy; I will betroth you to Me in faithfulness, and you shall know the LORD" (Hosea 2:19–20, NKJV).

This kind of spiritual intimacy brings joy both to us and to the Lord: "As a bridegroom rejoices over his bride, so will your God rejoice over you" (Isaiah 62:5, NIV).

The New Testament reminds us that Christ has made us His bride: "You too in the body of Christ have ended your relation to the law, so that you may be married to another husband, to Him who was raised from the dead, in order that we might bear fruit for God" (Romans 7:4, Williams).

THE BELONGINGNESS God provides means we can also accept with certainty that we're His friends.

"The friendship of the LORD is for those who fear him, and he makes known to them his covenant" (Psalm 25:14, ESV). In Christ, we can say of the Lord with confidence and joy, "This is my beloved and this is my friend" (Song of Solomon 5:16, NASB).

Jesus promises, "You are My friends if you do what I command you.... I have called you friends, for all things that I have heard from My Father I have made known to you" (John 15:14–15, NASB). And He says, "Look! Here I stand at the door and knock. If you hear me calling and open the door, I will come in, and we will share a meal as friends" (Revelation 3:20, NLT).

Your belongingness also means you can with certainty think of yourself as a citizen of God's heavenly kingdom. "It is your Father's good pleasure to give you the kingdom," Jesus said (Luke 12:32, ESV). Because of Christ, "Our citizenship is in heaven" (Philippians 3:20).

"Therefore let us be grateful for receiving a kingdom that cannot be shaken" (Hebrews 12:28, ESV). "For this world is not our home; we are looking forward to our city in heaven, which is yet to come" (Hebrews 13:14, NLT).

> By its nature, friendship revolves around common joys and interests, shared goals, and joint commitments.

> As a friend of God, what do you and He share in common?

> You are citizens along with all of God's holy people. You are members of God's family.
>
> EPHESIANS 2:19, NLT

YOUR BELONGINGNESS also means God accepts you as His servant. "You have been set free from sin and have become slaves of God" (Romans 6:22, ESV). "As the eyes of servants look to the hand of their masters...so our eyes look to the LORD our God" (Psalm 123:2, NKJV).

Christ set the example in this honor of serving God, for He "emptied Himself as He took on the form of a slave" (Philippians 2:7, Berkeley).

In your values and ways of thinking, why is it a great privilege for you to be a servant and worshiper of God?

As we serve our King on this earth by loving and helping other people, we can look forward to hearing Him say to us, "I was hungry, and you gave Me something to eat; I was thirsty, and you gave Me something to drink; I was a stranger, and you invited Me in; naked, and you clothed Me; I was sick, and you visited Me; I was in prison, and you came to Me" (Matthew 25:35–36, NASB).

Our belongingness also means that God accepts us as His true worshipers. This is made possible by our spiritual oneness with Christ, as He taught us: "True worshipers will worship the Father in spirit and truth; for such people the Father seeks to be His worshipers. God is spirit, and those who worship Him must worship in spirit and truth" (John 4:23–24, NASB). This is what God had promised His people long ages before: "I will give them one heart and mind to worship me forever.... I will put a desire in their hearts to worship me" (Jeremiah 32:39–40, NLT).

Bride, Friend,

My wonderful Lord, I thank You for Your intensely personal love that has actually invited me to take Your hand in marriage!

I have accepted Your proposal. And I know that You are and always will be entirely faithful to Your promise to betroth me to Yourself forever in righteousness and justice, in lovingkindness and mercy.

Allow the following passages to reinforce your personal calling as God's worshiper: I Chronicles 29:11–13; Psalms 95:6–7; 96:7–9; 145:1–3; Romans 12:1; Revelation 5:12.

I especially want to thank You for our friendship, a friendship in which You reveal so much to me and share so much with me—so many of Your plans and desires and promises and commitments… so much about Yourself and so much about me.

O Lord, my beloved King, thank You for gladly welcoming me into full citizenship in Your kingdom. Your promised kingdom is indeed my true and best homeland. May Your kingdom come!

And may I day by day find fresh delight in the many-sided belongingness I have with You.

WORTHY

WE HAVE A sense of worthiness when we feel we are persons of value because we're clean, good, and right. The opposite of worthiness is feeling guilty, disapproved, criticized, or condemned.

On the natural plane, we base our worthiness on how well we feel we live up to various ideals and standards—our own, or those of other people whose opinion we respect. Worthiness is also ours if we can easily feel forgiven by God and readily forgive ourselves when we fall short of the standards we believe in.

People of the world seek to gain a sense of being worthy or significant by taking pride in their natural strengths and abilities, and by seeking to feel superior to others in as many ways as they can. Or they wish they *could* feel proud and superior! Many people seek to elevate their low self-image by cutting others down or by associating with people they think are important.

The personal value we find in Christ frees us from these pursuits. It brings a whole new meaning to what worthiness is.

On the natural plane, where are you most tempted to look for a sense of personal worthiness?

WE CANNOT genuinely improve our sense of worthiness by simply deciding that we're okay—a decision based on human approval or reasoning. Rather we must first face up to negative and humbling truths about ourselves. Apart from Christ we are sinners. We've gone astray from God. We fall short of His glorious ideal. We're guilty before Him.

So the first step in becoming worthy is turning to God with the attitude, "God, be merciful to me a sinner!" (Luke 18:13, NKJV). Our position cannot be, "I *was* a sinner, but now I'm above that." Both in the unseen "recordings" in our unconscious mind and in their practical outworking in our lives, we still fall short of God's ideal. We never outgrow the need to pray, "LORD, be merciful to me; heal my soul, for I have sinned against You" (Psalm 41:4, NKJV).

Yet in our spirit, we've been impregnated with the life and righteousness of Christ because we've been born anew. We now share His worthiness. Although in the lower part of our being the "motions of sin" still stir, in the higher part we are righteous forever. Sin is no longer our nature or our master, and it no longer has any right to condemn us. Why? Because through trusting Christ we died out of the old life and were born into the new.

So we now can say, "In Christ, I'm all right as a person forever!"

How does coming before God with confession of sin seem to affect your love relationship with Him? How do you think *God* views it?

WE BELONG to God—and God never lightly values what He owns! He calls His people His "treasured possession" (Exodus 19:5, Psalm 135:4). That's what we are to Him. "The LORD's portion is his people"; we're "the apple of his eye" (Deuteronomy 32:9–10, ESV). "You are Mine," He tells us, and "you are precious in my eyes" (Isaiah 43:1, 4, ESV).

He treasures each of us as His created one: "It is He who has made us, and not we ourselves; we are His people and the sheep of His pasture" (Psalm 100:3, NKJV).

He also treasures and delights in each of us as His redeemed one: "God paid a ransom to save you…. And the ransom he paid was not mere gold or silver. He paid for you with the precious lifeblood of Christ, the sinless, spotless Lamb of God" (1 Peter 1:18–19, NLT). "He has purchased us to be his own people" (Ephesians 1:14, NLT).

No wonder Paul prays that "the eyes of our heart" will be flooded with light—with inner illumination—so that we will know "the riches of his glorious inheritance in the saints" (Ephesians 1:18, ESV). We are God's "gloriously rich portion" (1:18, Williams). "God has been made rich because we who are Christ's have been given to him!" (1:18, TLB).

This inheritance is mutual and relational. Out of His costly redemptive plan, *we* are what He gets, and *He* is what we get!

> "'They will be Mine,'
> says the LORD of hosts,
> 'on the day that I
> prepare My own
> possession.'"
>
> MALACHI 3:17, NASB

> "The Lord knows
> those who are His."
>
> 2 TIMOTHY 2:19, NKJV

As you meditate on God's Word, let Him reinforce in your heart the supporting pillar of your worthiness in His eyes.

Worthy

In You, my gracious Lord, I find true worthiness. Whenever I'm tempted to feel guilty or condemned or useless, I can come to You and Your truth. And I find the amazing fact that in Your eyes I'm highly valued, because Christ has made me clean and forgiven and good and right in my innermost being—in my true self.

Forgive me for the many times I seek a sense of worth from my natural abilities and traits, or by belittling others to make myself look better by comparison. Enable me instead to seek my sense of worth from You.

The worth You provide me in Christ is amazing—and all the more so as I face the fact of my natural sinfulness and weakness. Thank You for rescuing me when I was deeply entrenched in spiritual deadness and lack of power, and for resurrecting me to true significance and growing Christlikeness.

Thank You for assuring me that You treasure me, that I am precious in Your eyes because You created me—and even more because You redeemed me at the cost of Your Son's precious blood.

Take note of the question about value or worth that Jesus asks in Matthew 6:26, "Are you not worth much more...?" In this chapter on being worthy, what statements most help you answer that question personally, for yourself?

Loved

"The God of love and peace will be with you."

2 CORINTHIANS 13:11, NKJV

"In order to satisfy the great and wonderful and intense love with which He loved us,...He made us alive together in fellowship and in union with Christ."

EPHESIANS 2:4–5, AMP

"'With everlasting love I will have compassion on you,' says the LORD, your Redeemer."

ISAIAH 54:8, ESV

WE UNDERSTAND our worthiness most clearly by looking in the mirror of God's love for us.

His Word invites us to fully behold this love: "See how very much our heavenly Father loves us" (1 John 3:1, NLT).

His love is limitless. He assures us, "My love will know no bounds" (Hosea 14:4, NLT).

His love for us is also permanent: "Nothing can ever separate us from his love. Death can't, and life can't. The angels can't, and the demons can't. Our fears for today, our worries about tomorrow, and even the powers of hell can't keep God's love away. Whether we are high above the sky or in the deepest ocean, nothing in all creation will ever be able to separate us from the love of God that is revealed in Christ Jesus our Lord" (Romans 8:38–39, NLT).

God is love.

1 JOHN 4:8

Many waters cannot quench love.

SONG OF SOLOMON 8:7

AGAIN AND AGAIN the Lord assures us of His love. "You are precious in my eyes...and I love you" (Isaiah 43:4, ESV). "My steadfast love shall not depart from you" (Isaiah 54:10, ESV). "I have loved you with an everlasting love; therefore I have continued my faithfulness to you" (Jeremiah 31:3, ESV).

Jesus says, "The Father tenderly loves you... As the Father loved Me, I also have loved you; abide in My love" (John 16:27, Williams; 15:9, NKJV).

God's love gives us lasting confidence. We can "know and rely on the love God has for us" (1 John 4:16, NIV).

One of Paul's deepest prayers urges us to deeply experience this love: "May your roots go down deep into the soil of God's marvelous love; and may you be able to feel and understand, as all God's children should, how long, how wide, how deep, and how high his love really is; and to experience this love for yourselves, though it is so great that you will never see the end of it or fully know or understand it" (Ephesians 3:17–19, TLB).

> "The Father Himself loves you, since you have loved Me and have believed that I came from the Father."
>
> JOHN 16:27, BERKELEY

> God proves His love for us by the fact that Christ died for us.
>
> ROMANS 5:8, WILLIAMS

"Listen to Him, my children. He speaks to you, He teaches you in a thousand ways every day. Through the love of those who love you and live to help you, He touches you, and He speaks to you. In the sunrise and sunset, and in the moonlight, through the loneliness of the things that He has made, through the thousand joys that He plans for every one of you, through the sorrows that come too, in all these things, through all these things, He who loved you unto death is speaking to you. Listen; do not be deaf and blind to Him, and as you keep quiet and listen, you will know deep down in your heart that you are loved."

AMY CARMICHAEL

OUT OF GOD'S intense and endless love for us comes both His desire and His promise to stay near to us at all times, in all circumstances. "I brought you to myself," He says (Exodus 19:4, NLT). "The one the LORD loves rests between his shoulders" (Deuteronomy 33:12, NIV). He is at home within us, and He surrounds us all day long.

And He promises, "When you pass through the waters, I will be with you" (Isaiah 43:2). "I will not forget you" (Isaiah 49:15, NKJV).

"Remember," Jesus says, "I am with you all the days until the end of the age" (Matthew 28:20, Berkeley). "I will not leave you orphans," He promises; "I will come to you" (John 14:18, NKJV).

The Lord stays near to us to dine with us in the intimate fellowship enjoyed by dearest friends. "Our fellowship is with the Father and with His Son Jesus Christ" (1 John 1:3, NKJV).

Therefore with loving confidence that thrills the Lord's heart, we can gladly acknowledge His nearness: "I will fear no evil; for You are with me" (Psalm 23:4, NKJV). "In the shadow of Your wings I will make my refuge" (Psalm 57:1, NKJV). "I am continually with You; You hold me by my right hand" (Psalm 73:23, NKJV).

And to those around us we can testify, "He has brought me to his banquet hall, and his banner over me is love" (Song of Solomon 2:4, NASB).

> "In Christ Jesus you who once were far off have been brought near by the blood of Christ."
>
> EPHESIANS 2:13, NKJV

> The Lord paid an infinite price to gain intimacy with you.

Loved

Thank You, Lord, that You have given me Your perfect love as my
dwelling place—as my home, where my heart can be at rest.
In Your wondrous love, I find a hiding place—
a haven that I never want to leave!

You are my Beloved, and I rest my head on Your shoulder, thankful
that You will never abandon me, that You will never let me go.
You'll never let anything separate me from Your
measureless love revealed in Christ Jesus my Lord.

You've given Your Word that You will never withhold Your love from
me. Instead, You will lavish it on me more and more in all the ages to
come! How I praise and adore You! Your limitless and eternal love is
beyond description. Yet I cannot help but voice my praise to You
for surrounding me now and forever with Your boundless love.

Father, I rejoice in the mirror of Your love where I can see so
accurately who I truly am! As my days on earth pass by,
continue to make me more aware of Your vast love for me—
and more upheld and overwhelmed by it.

Listen for the Lord's voice calling personally to you in these passages about His love for you and your love for Him: Deuteronomy 30:6; 33:12; Psalms 18:1; 94:18; 116:1; Matthew 22:37; John 3:16; 14:21; Romans 5:5; 1 Peter 1:8; 1 John 4:18

DELIGHTED IN, fAVORED, AND HONORED

THE MORE we realize what a source of pleasure we are to God, the more His perfect love will continually reinforce our sense of worth. "Because of what Christ has done we have become gifts to God that he delights in" (Ephesians 1:11, TLB). "For the LORD takes pleasure in His people" (Psalm 149:4, NASB).

How does it make you feel to know that you actually bring delight and pleasure to God's heart?

God wants us to know that He rejoices over us with great gladness and exults over us by singing a happy song (Zephaniah 3:17, NLT). He delights in us! (Isaiah 62:4, NKJV).

As we realize this truth, we learn to hear Him whisper, "You have captivated my heart" (Song of Solomon 4:9, ESV).

Out of His delight in us springs an endless flow of favor. "The LORD bestows favor and honor. No good thing does he withhold from those who walk uprightly" (Psalm 84:11, ESV). He says to each of us, "I have known you by name, and you have also found favor in My sight" (Exodus 33:12, NASB).

THE MORE we receive the grace—the unmerited favor—that God pours out on us in Christ, the more we will want to exclaim, "Look how the Eternal marks me out for favor!" (Psalm 4:3, Moffatt). "For surely, O LORD, you bless the righteous; you surround them with your favor as with a shield" (Psalm 5:12, NIV).

His favor includes showing His appreciation for specific things we do in serving Him—even small things—and His promise to reward us for them. "God is not so unjust as to forget the work you have done and the love you have shown His name in the service you have rendered for your fellow-Christians, and still are doing" (Hebrews 6:10, Williams). "Nothing you do for the Lord is ever useless" (1 Corinthians 15:58, NLT).

Paul tells us, "Whatever good anyone does, this he will receive back from the Lord" (Ephesians 6:8, ESV). And Jesus said, "Whoever gives one of these little ones only a cup of cold water in the name of a disciple, assuredly, I say to you, he shall by no means lose his reward" (Matthew 10:42, NKJV).

Therefore in all the labor we do for Him, we can say with confidence, "I will trust God for my reward" (Isaiah 49:4, NLT).

> "I will make an everlasting covenant with them: I will never stop doing good to them."
>
> JEREMIAH 32:40, NIV

"Surely there is a reward for the righteous."

PSALM 58:11, NKJV

Tell the righteous it will be well with them, for they will enjoy the fruit of their deeds.

ISAIAH 3:10, NIV

> "He withdraws not His eyes from the righteous (the upright in right standing with God); but He sets them forever with kings upon the throne, and they are exalted."
>
> JOB 36:7, AMP

> "Jesus promised, 'I will invite everyone who is victorious to sit with me on my throne, just as I was victorious and sat with my Father on his throne.'"
>
> REVELATION 3:21, NLT

> "We are honored in God's sight!"
>
> ISAIAH 43:4

GOD HONORS us by making us royalty in Christ—sons and daughters of the King of kings. Jesus Himself "has made us kings" (Revelation 1:6, NKJV). We who are alive with Christ's righteousness can now live all our lives like kings! (Romans 5:17, Phillips).

What a high privilege! What an exalted position!

Before we knew Christ, we were spiritual paupers, needing to fight for our own rights and push our way through life. We were clothed in various kinds of rags—such as whining, coaxing, self-pity, anger, resentment, revenge. We tried to borrow from others the kind of love we desperately needed—discovering too often that they were paupers too!

We went through garbage pails looking for scraps of self-realization. We tried to find an identity that we could accept, a feeling that we were truly and unshakably somebody important. We tried to elbow our way to the top of the ash heap of visible status. We sought for a position above (or at least equal to) someone we were competing with. Or we just sat at the bottom of the heap, resenting those who were higher up.

The attitudes that are accepted and even expected of paupers or beggars are unbecoming to royalty—and unnecessary. We can now be liberated from them, because our King holds us in highest favor. He promises to look out for our welfare and our true rights, to defend us, to work things out for us.

Delighted In,

Dear Father, how glad I am that You not only love me—You also like me. You find delight and pleasure in me, and You created me for the very purpose of bringing You both pleasure and glory. Show me how to fulfill that purpose more and more.

I worship You as my King—as the King of kings—and I give You thanks for calling me out of this fallen world and bringing me into Your Kingdom and Your family. As a royal child, You invite me into Your throne room, to spend time with You there. And You assure me of access to Your throne forever and ever.

I rejoice in the never-ending flow of favor and honor that You send from your heart to mine. Thank You for the rewards You promise for loving obedience on my part—for good deeds that are simply an extension of Your never-ending grace—and rewards that help display Your attribute of always being a Giver.

How grateful I am that in Christ I never need to live as a pauper, not even for a moment. Thank You for delivering me from spiritual poverty and shame into Your very own royal richness and honor!

Use these passages to reflect further on your royal and honored status in God's eyes:
1 Samuel 2:8;
Psalm 91:15;
Luke 7:28;
John 17:22;
2 Timothy 2:12, 20–21;
1 Peter 1:7

Favored, and Honored

NURtuReD, satisfieD, aND secuRe

As we know God better, and realize that we are His treasured possession in Christ, we're able to trust Him more for His personal and compassionate care. Because He's so rich—with unlimited resources—we can live free from anxiety, knowing that our every need will be fully met. And when anxiety overtakes us, we have in Christ the solution.

> "God…is so rich in mercy on account of the great love He has for us."
>
> EPHESIANS 2:4, WILLIAMS

"We are the people he watches over, the sheep under his care" (Psalm 95:7, NLT). "He will feed His flock like a shepherd" (Isaiah 40:11, NKJV). And He feeds us "with the finest of wheat; and with honey from the rock" (Psalm 81:16, NKJV).

> Why is anxiety so wrong and so harmful to us—and so unneccessary?

"He cares for you" (1 Peter 5:7, NKJV), and therefore "You can throw the whole weight of your anxieties upon him, for you are his personal concern" (1 Peter 5:7, Phillips). Jesus promised us on behalf of His Father: "He will give you all you need from day to day if you live for him and make the Kingdom of God your primary concern" (Matthew 6:33, NLT).

God will supply every need of yours according to his riches in glory in Christ Jesus.

PHILIPPIANS 4:19, ESV

GOD IS CONSTANT and thorough and deliberate in His care for us. He speaks of His people as His vineyard and says, "I, the LORD, am its keeper; every moment I water it.... I keep it night and day" (Isaiah 27:3, ESV). He tells us, "I, the LORD, made you, and I will not forget to help you" (Isaiah 44:21, NLT). "I made you, and I will care for you" (Isaiah 46:4, NLT). So He keeps inviting us to taste and see that He is good (Psalm 34:8).

Every day in unique ways we experience the Lord's care and nurture, for "His tender compassions...are new every morning" (Lamentations 3:22–23, AMP). The Lord "satisfies you with good so that your youth is renewed like the eagle's" (Psalm 103:5, ESV).

The Bible promises that Jesus, as the church's Bridegroom, "nourishes and cherishes" us (Ephesians 5:29, NKJV). Therefore we can say with contentment, "The LORD is my shepherd, I shall not be in want" (Psalm 23:1, NIV).

"My people," He promises, "will be satisfied with My goodness" (Jeremiah 31:14, NASB). So we can affirm to Him that we are abundantly satisfied with the fullness of His house as we gladly drink from the river of His pleasures (Psalm 36:8, NKJV). We can tell Him, "You satisfy me more than the richest of foods. I will praise you with songs of joy" (Psalm 63:5, NLT).

"I am the good shepherd."
JOHN 10:11, NKJV

"Forget not all his benefits, who forgives all your iniquity, who heals all your diseases, who redeems your life from the pit, who crowns you with steadfast love and mercy."
PSALM 103:2–4, ESV

"He satisfies the longing soul, and fills the hungry soul with goodness."
PSALM 107:9, NKJV

GOD ALSO PROMISES that, as we let Him be our God and King, He will be our Refuge and Champion and Protector. Therefore we will be secure.

"Yes," He assures us, "I will help you, I will uphold you with My righteous right hand" (Isaiah 41:10, NKJV). "For He Himself has said, *I will never leave you nor forsake you*" (Hebrews 13:5, NKJV).

In His sovereign care we're guarded from every threat and unmet need! "The God of all grace, who has called you to his eternal glory in Christ, will himself restore, confirm, strengthen, and establish you" (1 Peter 5:10, ESV). "The Lord is faithful, and he will strengthen and protect you from the evil one" (2 Thessalonians 3:3, NIV). He "is able to keep you from stumbling, and to make you stand in the presence of His glory blameless with great joy" (Jude 1:24, NASB).

Therefore we can say, "My help comes from the LORD" (Psalm 121:2). "Blessed be the Lord, who daily bears us up" (Psalm 68:19, ESV). "In peace I will both lie down and sleep, for You alone, O LORD, make me to dwell in safety" (Psalm 4:8, NASB).

With David we can testify of God, "He only is my rock and my salvation, my stronghold; I shall not be greatly shaken" (Psalm 62:2, NASB).

> Though he stumble, he will not fall, for the LORD upholds him with his hand.
>
> PSALM 37:24, NIV

"The Lord is good, a Strength and Stronghold in the day of trouble; He knows (recognizes, has knowledge of, and understands) those who take refuge and trust in Him."

NAHUM 1:7, AMP

"He...set my feet upon a rock, making my steps secure."

PSALM 40:2, ESV

"The eternal God is your refuge, and underneath are the everlasting arms."

DEUTERONOMY 33:27, NKJV

Nurtured, Satisfied,

O Lord my Shepherd, I worship You as the One who perfectly cares for me, so that I never need to be anxious.

You nurture me and satisfy me with good things, continually refreshing and renewing my life. For these endless gifts of Your grace, Lord, I thank You with a joyful heart.
"I will rejoice and be glad in Your lovingkindness"
(Psalm 31:7, NASB).

I also praise You and worship You for being my Strength, my Champion, my Defender. Thank You for the limitless power and wisdom that You bring to bear on my problems and difficulties. You truly are "an ever-present help in trouble" (Psalm 46:1, NIV).

Therefore, Lord, I can affirm with Paul, "I know whom I have trusted and I am absolutely sure that He is able to guard what I have entrusted to Him" (2 Timothy 1:12, Williams).
And Lord, I choose to trust You, as Paul did, to guard and rescue me from every danger, and to bring me safely home into Your eternal kingdom (2 Timothy 4:18, ESV).

The Lord's faithful nurturing means that we can fully rest in His presence and care.

What encouragement about His promised rest do you find in these verses?
Psalms 23:2; 37:7; 62:1; 116:7;
Isaiah 28:12; 30:15; 32:18;
Jeremiah 6:16;
Matthew 11:28–29

and Secure

competent

"For we realize that our life in this world is actually his life lived in us."

I John 4:17, Phillips

On the natural plane, in what ways are you most tempted to focus on your own sense of personal competence or incompetence, instead of relying on Christ's life within you?

IN ADDITION to the new belongingness and worthiness we experience in Christ, we also gain a new sense of competence.

On a limited human plane, we often base our feeling of competence on our abilities and successes, and especially on how we feel others view us. We're afraid we won't meet their expectations of us.

But as we take hold of our new identity in Christ and His more-than-adequate presence within us, we find in Him our complete sufficiency. We can say with Paul, "Our sufficiency is from God" (2 Corinthians 3:5, NKJV).

The more we meditate on this truth, the more it dawns on us that righteous, holy living is consistent with the persons we now are. It isn't something foreign to us that we have to produce out of duty or even gratefulness. Rather, as we choose to follow Christ, we can expect to live a holy life because of who *Christ* is, what He has done, and what He has made us through our new birth. Our competence is the outflow of His life in us.

OUR SENSE of competence will be continually enriched as we realize that the Holy Spirit within us is continually at work to transform us. No matter what faults and personal struggles we now face, we can cultivate this thought pattern: *"I can change!* I can become more than I am. I can develop a greater ability to cope with life, and especially to relate to other people in a more positive and significant way."

This is true because we *are* changing. As we behold the Lord, "All of us…are being transformed into likeness to Him, from one degree of splendor to another, since it comes from the Lord who is the Spirit" (2 Corinthians 3:18, Williams).

This change in us—this Christian growth and transformation—rests from beginning to end on the loving work of God within us. "He Himself works in you and accomplishes that which is pleasing in His sight, through Jesus Christ" (Hebrews 13:21, AMP).

Relational truths that belonged to God's people in the Old Testament now apply to us. The Lord sees us through eyes of love as a bridegroom sees his bride, focusing on the positives. Each of us is uniquely beautiful in His sight and our face is lovely (Song of Solomon 2:14). "How beautiful you are, my love," He says, "how lovely in that which delights!" (Song of Solomon 7:6, Berkeley). And as we grow spiritually and delight in the Lord's perfections, the beauty we have from Him continues to deepen and intensify. "You will also be a crown of beauty in the hand of the LORD, and a royal diadem in the hand of your God" (Isaiah 62:3, NASB).

> "The one thing I ask of the LORD—the thing I seek most—is to live in the house of the LORD all the days of my life, delighting in the LORD's perfections."
>
> PSALM 27:4, NLT

SO WE CAN be confident that the best is yet to come as we let God work in our personalities and our actions.

"For because of our faith, he has brought us into this place of highest privilege where we now stand, and we confidently and joyfully look forward to actually becoming all that God has had in mind for us to be" (Romans 5:2, TLB). "For we are God's masterpiece. He has created us anew in Christ Jesus, so that we can do the good things he planned for us long ago" (Ephesians 2:10, NLT).

What important training and discipline and refinement is God taking you through now?

As the Lord continually trains, teaches, refines, and disciplines us, we'll more and more fulfill our God-designed destiny as His masterpieces.

"For the Lord disciplines the one he loves" (Hebrews 12:6, ESV). Along the way, He doesn't expect from us perfect performance or an "ideal" personality, nor does He condemn us for our failures. "For He knows our frame; He remembers that we are dust" (Psalm 103:14, NKJV). What He expects from you and me is realistic. He holds before us high, challenging goals in holiness and righteousness, and He helps us measure up to them. With Paul we can say, "Not that I have already obtained this or am already perfect, but I press on to make it my own, because Christ Jesus has made me his own.... I press on toward the goal for the prize of the upward call of God in Christ Jesus" (Philippians 3:12, 14, ESV).

Competent

I praise You, Lord God, that through my new birth in Christ You have begun to make me competent and adequate for the future You have planned for me. In all that You are, I can find complete sufficiency for all that awaits me.

Thank You for Your promise to transform me from one degree of glory to another. I rejoice that I will be more and more pleasing to You, more beautiful in Your eyes, more conformed to Your eternal purposes for me.

Yes, the best is yet to come! I look forward with confidence to what You will accomplish in me and through me.

Thank You especially for loving me enough to discipline and train me, and for the high, challenging goals and standards You call me to. How good to know that You will empower me to reach them— "Not that I am sufficient of myself to think anything as being from myself, but my sufficiency is from You" (2 Corinthians 3:5, NKJV, personalized).

David said, "You teach me wisdom in the inmost place" (Psalm 51:6, NIV).

What do the following verses indicate about the personal program of training and discipline which the Lord has in store for you—to teach you "wisdom in the inmost place"? Psalms 25:8–9; 118:18; 119:67, 71, 75; Isaiah 48:10; Matthew 11:29; John 15:2; Romans 5:3–4; Hebrews 12:7–13

BOLD AND CONFIDENT

OUR COMPETENCE in Christ brings us new freedom and power. It makes us bold to do His will.

It's our privilege to experience a basic breakthrough into freedom from "ought to" living into the joy of simply living out Christ's life—of letting Him display His life in and through us. He grants us freedom from sin's crippling restraints: "You are free by God's grace.... You are free from sin, your old master" (Romans 6:14, 18, NLT).

Our freedom is Spirit produced and Spirit sustained, for "the Lord is the Spirit, and wherever the Spirit of the Lord is, he gives freedom" (2 Corinthians 3:17, NLT). "For the life-giving principles of the Spirit have freed you in Christ Jesus from the control of the principles of sin and death" (Romans 8:2, Berkeley).

Therefore with boldness we can tell the Lord, "O LORD, truly I am your servant...you have freed me from my chains.... I run in the path of your commands, for you have set my heart free.... I will walk about in freedom, for I have sought out your precepts" (Psalms 116:16; 119:32, 45, NIV).

"For he breaks down gates of bronze and cuts through bars of iron."

PSALM 107:16, NIV

"For freedom Christ has set us free; stand firm therefore, and do not submit again to a yoke of slavery."

GALATIANS 5:1, ESV

WE CAN BE bold because we are on the winning side! In Christ, strength and triumph are ours, and we no longer have to yield to defeatism. "God...always leads us in triumph in Christ" (2 Corinthians 2:14, NKJV).

It's not that we don't face trials and spiritual conflicts. But in Christ we are guaranteed victory. "Therefore we do not lose heart. Though outwardly we are wasting away, yet inwardly we are being renewed day by day" (2 Corinthians 4:16, NIV).

"Overwhelming victory is ours through Christ, who loved us" (Romans 8:37, NLT). We are overcomers because He who is in us is greater than he who is in the world (1 John 4:4, NKJV). We've been born of God, and "whatever is born of God overcomes the world" (1 John 5:4, NKJV).

"We can say with confidence, 'The Lord is my helper, so I will not be afraid'" (Hebrews 13:6, NLT). We can affirm, "It is God who arms me with strength, and makes my way perfect" (Psalm 18:32, NKJV), and "I am ready for anything through the strength of the one who lives within me" (Philippians 4:13, Phillips).

So we praise the Lord by telling Him personally, "You encourage me by giving me the strength I need" (Psalm 138:3, NLT). "My heart is confident, O God; my heart is confident" (Psalm 57:7, Berkeley).

"As you live this new life, we pray that you will be strengthened from God's boundless resources, so that you will find yourselves able to pass through any experience and endure it with courage."

COLOSSIANS 1:11, PHILLIPS

"The eyes of the LORD search the whole earth in order to strengthen those whose hearts are fully committed to him."

2 CHRONICLES 16:9, NLT

OUR BOLDNESS springs from a quiet confidence in God's guidance and instruction as He leads us into a life of true wisdom.

"For the LORD gives wisdom" (Proverbs 2:6). "He leads the humble in what is right, and teaches the humble his way" (Psalm 25:9, ESV). "He will show them the path they should choose" (Psalm 25:12, NLT).

He grants us this guidance in personal ways as we hear Him tell us, "I am the LORD your God, who teaches you what is best for you, who directs you in the way you should go" (Isaiah 48:17, NIV). "I will guide you along the best pathway for your life. I will advise you and watch over you" (Psalm 32:8, NLT). "Your ears shall hear a word behind you, saying, 'This is the way, walk in it,' whenever you turn to the right hand or whenever you turn to the left" (Isaiah 30:21, NKJV).

It's not that following the Lord ever gets simple and easy. But there is a kind of inner simplicity that we all need to cultivate more fully. It grows within us as we learn to depend more constantly on the indwelling life of Christ, counting on Him for wisdom and strength.

"For the LORD will be your confidence."
PROVERBS 3:26, ESV

"We put no confidence in human effort. Instead, we boast about what Christ Jesus has done for us."
PHILIPPIANS 3:3, NLT

"Your confidence...has great reward."
HEBREWS 10:35, NKJV

Bold and Confident

Lord God, You are my Liberator and Savior. Thank You for setting me free from the disabling power of sin and death, and giving me a life of fresh, new boldness in You. Help me to rise up and soar ever higher in this new liberty. I know that the more I give You the controls of my life, the freer I will be.

As I consider how limited and vulnerable I am, how encouraging it is to hear You say, "My grace is sufficient for you, for My strength is made perfect in weakness"! In new ways may Your power rest upon me and govern me, so I can say with confidence, "When I am weak, then I am strong" (2 Corinthians 12:9–10).

Reflect on what these passages say to your heart about the Lord's promised guidance for you:
Matthew 11:25;
John 6:45; 14:26;
James 1:5;
1 John 2:20, 27

Thank You that I'm on the winning side; I'm an eternal victor with You. I can face the future with boldness and without fear, knowing that You will give the strength I need to be an overcomer in any trial that comes my way.

Thank You especially for Your wise and trustworthy guidance, as day by day You lead me in paths of righteousness for Your name's sake.

Father, enable me to stand on these truths boldly and consistently, with an ever-growing confidence in You.

PURPOSEFUL

OUR SENSE of competence is strongly reinforced by the highly significant purposes that become ours as we learn to bring glory to God.

The Lord tells us, "You are my servant…and you will bring me glory" (Isaiah 49:3, NLT). We bring Him glory by serving as channels of His love and grace to the people our lives touch.

His Word tells us, "Live a life of love" (Ephesians 5:2, NIV), and the love we ourselves have received from Him motivates us to obey this command. "Dear friends, since God loved us that much, we surely ought to love each other" (1 John 4:11, NLT). "We love, because He first loved us" (1 John 4:19, NASB). Serving others is not a grueling obligation but a high and special calling.

We hear the Lord asking, "Do you love Me?… Do you love Me?… Do you love Me?" (John 21:15–17, NKJV). In our daily lives, we answer "Yes" by sharing His love with others.

"If you keep yourself pure, you will be a utensil God can use for his purpose. Your life will be clean, and you will be ready for the Master to use you for every good work."

2 TIMOTHY 2:21, NLT

THE LORD Himself enables us to reach others with His love: "Now you can have sincere love for each other as brothers and sisters because you were cleansed from your sins" (1 Peter 1:22, NLT). He's always our Teacher of love. "You yourselves have been personally taught by God to love one another" (1 Thessalonians 4:9, AMP). The very freedom we have in the Spirit is a freedom to love—"For you have been called to live in freedom...freedom to serve one another in love" (Galatians 5:13, NLT).

Paul's prayers help us envision the wide possibilities of loving others: "May the Lord make you to increase and excel and overflow in love for one another and for all people" (1 Thessalonians 3:12, AMP); "that your love may overflow still more and more, directed by fuller knowledge and keener insight" (Philippians 1:9, Williams).

> "Let your good deeds shine out for all to see, so that everyone will praise your heavenly Father."
>
> MATTHEW 5:16, NLT

Such love is the driving force behind our calling as witnesses for Christ to both believers and unbelievers. "The love of Christ controls and urges and impels us, because we are of the opinion and conviction that...One died for all... so that all those who live might live no longer to and for themselves, but to and for Him Who died and was raised again for their sake" (2 Corinthians 5:14, AMP). We don't all have the gift of evangelism, but we all have the privilege of influencing others for Christ.

> "God deliberately chose things the world considers foolish in order to shame those who think they are wise. And he chose those who are powerless to shame those who are powerful."
>
> I CORINTHIANS 1:27, NLT

> "'You are My witnesses,' says the LORD, 'and My servant whom I have chosen.'"
>
> ISAIAH 43:10, NKJV

FROM CHRIST'S presence within us, God wants to manifest through us the fragrance that results from knowing Him (2 Corinthians 2:14, Berkeley).

Why do we qualify for this exciting privilege? Only because we are in Christ and He is in us. "It has pleased God to reveal His Son in me," wrote Paul in Galatians 1:15–16. "It is He Who has qualified us—making us to be fit and worthy and sufficient—as ministers and dispensers of a new covenant of salvation through Christ" (2 Corinthians 3:6, AMP).

How do we, with our assortment of inadequacies, fulfill our high calling as witnesses for Christ? Not by trying to be what we're not, but by realizing who we are in Christ and then depending on Him to let our true inner self shine forth.

We're not qualified from a human viewpoint, for we lack many longed-for qualities, abilities, and talents. Yet from God's viewpoint we are qualified. "The LORD does not see as man sees; for man looks at the outward appearance, but the LORD looks at the heart" (1 Samuel 16:7, NKJV).

Purposeful

⤨⤨⤨

I worship and praise You, Lord God, for including me in Your glorious eternal purposes. Thank You for the thrilling sense of significance this gives to me—the assurance that in Your service I can live a life of love and adventure and fruitfulness. Thank You for the part I can share in communicating to others Your exciting plans and purposes.

Thank You especially for the incredible freedom You give me to truly love others. Keep refining me as a channel of Your supernatural love flowing freely to those around me.

I exult in knowing that You allow me to be Your witness and Your ambassador. Keep refining and humbling me so that Your life and message will come through more and more clearly in my actions and words. May my service be unhindered by self-centeredness or lack of sensitivity. Let others sense Your fragrant aroma in me.

Thank You for the fulfilling purposes You have given me. May they keep me from pursuing a sense of purpose in the wrong way, by looking to the wrong sources instead of looking to You.

Jesus spoke of "those who hear the word, accept it, and *bear fruit*" (Mark 4:20, NKJV, emphasis mine). What does He have in mind for you as a bearer of fruit for Him? Reflect deeply on His words in John 15, verses 2, 4, 5, 8, and 16. Then answer the above question as fully as you can.

And what does the Lord have in mind for you as His soldier? Explore that topic in these passages:
2 Corinthians 10:3–5;
Ephesians 6:11–18;
1 Timothy 6:12;
2 Timothy 2:3

embracing a glorious future

WE CAN KEEP our sense of competence strong by remembering that God is always at work in us. His working means we are becoming like mighty oaks, "the planting of the LORD, that he may be glorified" (Isaiah 61:3, ESV). And we are like a field where He plants His crops, or like a building He constructs (1 Corinthians 3:9). We are like clay in the hands of God, the master potter (Isaiah 64:8).

"Only God...gives the growth."

1 CORINTHIANS 3:7, ESV

God wants us to cooperate with Him in His work of training us and building us up. He wants us to continually choose to be His disciples—His dedicated followers and learners. Then we can faithfully affirm with joyful gratitude, "You will keep on guiding me with your counsel, leading me to a glorious destiny" (Psalm 73:24, NLT).

"O Lord our God... we rely on you."

2 CHRONICLES 14:11, ESV

WE CAN BE fully confident in how the Lord shapes our circumstances, both present and future. He assures us that "to those who love God, who are called according to his plan, everything that happens fits into a pattern for good" (Romans 8:28, Phillips).

Counting on God's good plan fills us with hope, for we know that ultimately, in the ages to come, it will mean perfect holiness—complete freedom from all sinful acts and attitudes. We will be totally set apart for God for all eternity.

In our innermost being Christ's sacrifice has already made us "forever perfect" (Hebrews 10:14, TLB). In Him, our holiness is something we've already received: "We have been made holy (consecrated and sanctified) through the offering made once for all of the body of Jesus Christ (the Anointed One)" (Hebrews 10:10, AMP). Meanwhile we continue to experience this holiness as the Lord keeps on working in our daily lives, conforming our mind, our emotions, and our will to the image of Christ.

> "He will keep you strong to the end, so that you will be blameless on the day of our Lord Jesus Christ."
>
> 1 CORINTHIANS 1:8, NIV

Again Paul's prayers envision the reality that is ours to grow into: "Now may the God of peace himself sanctify you completely, and may your whole spirit and soul and body be kept blameless at the coming of our Lord Jesus Christ. He who calls you is faithful; he will surely do it" (1 Thessalonians 5:23–24, ESV). So we can look to the Lord as Paul did, counting on Him to "strengthen and confirm and establish our hearts faultlessly pure and unblamable in holiness in the sight of our God and Father" (1 Thessalonians 3:13, AMP, personalized).

> "The LORD has set apart the godly for himself."
>
> PSALM 4:3, ESV

IN GOD'S unlimited view, He sees our increasing glory as His Spirit transforms us into finished works of art. He promises that "He who has begun a good work in you will bring it to completion in the day of Christ Jesus" (Philippians 1:6 Berkeley). He Himself will put the finishing touches on us (2 Corinthians 5:5, Williams).

So we can say with confidence, "The LORD will fulfill his purpose for me" (Psalm 138:8, ESV). We can count on His promise, "Surely you have a future ahead of you; your hope will not be disappointed" (Proverbs 23:17–18, NLT).

Our hope will be perfectly fulfilled on that day when our Lord will be revealed to us in all His glory. We will finally be all that Christ Jesus saved us for and longs for us to be (Philippians 3:12, NLT). That day "will mean splendor unimaginable. It will be a breath-taking wonder to all who believe" (2 Thessalonians 1:10, Phillips). An eternal weight of glory is awaiting us (2 Corinthians 4:17, ESV).

We will see this glory shining from the face of our Lord Himself, for He has promised, "Your eyes will see the King in His beauty" (Isaiah 33:17, NKJV). And He will share with us His matchless glory: "We know that when He appears, we will be like Him, because we will see Him just as He is" (1 John 3:2, NASB).

> "Thou art what I obtain from life, O Thou Eternal; Thou Thyself art my share. Fair prospects are allotted me; a blissful heritage is mine."
>
> PSALM 16:5–6, MOFFATT

> "As for me, I shall behold your face in righteousness... I shall be satisfied with your likeness."
>
> PSALM 17:15, ESV

Embracing a Glorious

My loving God, how I praise and adore You for being constantly at work to fulfill Your gracious purposes in me. Every day is alive with Your fresh acts of mercy as You move me forward in fulfilling Your plans for my life.

You are my Lord and Master, and I commit myself to You as Your disciple—as your dedicated follower. Help me to keep choosing the path of discipleship day by day. May I constantly yield to Your Word and Your patient counsel and take to heart the lessons You want me to learn.

Thank You for Your good purposes which undergird all that happens to me. I'm especially grateful to know that You are leading me on the path to perfect holiness, to full freedom from the presence of sin in the eternal glory You have called me to. And I praise You for the blend of trials and blessings that You are using to prepare me to reign with You forever.

How I rejoice in Your plans to bring me to glory, where I will enjoy splendor unimaginable and unending. And most of all, I will see You face to face. You have promised me the supreme privilege of "beholding the King in His beauty." I will see You just as You are…and I will be forever satisfied.

To deepen your personal hope in all that God has promised you for eternity, reflect on these passages: Psalm 16:11; Romans 8:18, 23; 1 Corinthians 15:54; 2 Corinthians 5:1; Ephesians 1:9–10; Colossians 1:27; Titus 2:13; 1 Peter 1:13

Future

It will be worth it all,
When we see Jesus;
Life's trials will seem so small
When we see Christ.
One glimpse of His dear face
All sorrow will erase.
So bravely run the race
'Til we see Christ. *

* Words by Esther Rusthoi; copyright 1941
by Esther Kerr Rusthoi, Al Smith, owner.

acknowledgments

I'm deeply indebted to Thomas Womack, my favorite editor for many years. He went beyond the call of duty in selecting the topics to be covered and organizing the first draft of this book. My part was simply making notes on the subjects for years and polishing the material. He's a great gift from the Lord!

I also want to thank Sharon Linquist, my dear friend and secretary, for her excellent work behind the scenes, inputting revision after revision and lending her ear as I bounced off ideas. She enabled me to have the time to get this material ready to be published.

I'm also indebted to those who have used the *31 Days* series. They have motivated me to write this book on my favorite topic—our delightful, all-sufficient Lord and who we are through our inner union with Him.

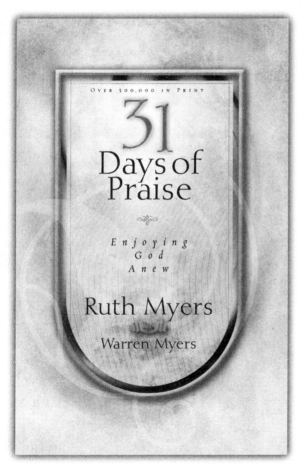

31 DAYS TO A MORE POWERFUL PRAYER LIFE

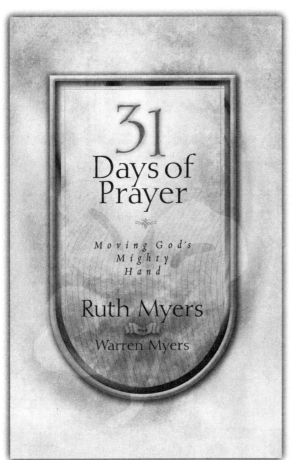

It takes but a few weeks to form a habit. *31 Days of Prayer* can help you form a rich prayer habit that lasts a lifetime with this beautiful and practical devotional.

Authors Ruth and Warren Myers will show you how to grow in prayer, even if the amount of time set aside seems small at first. *31 Days of Prayer* will lead you step by step into praying about what is close to your heart and to God's.

31 Days of Prayer
ISBN 1-57673-874-4